Introduction to Rug Hooking

A Beginner's Guide to Tools, Techniques, and Materials

By Kris Miller

Published by
AMPRY PUBLISHING LLC
3400 Dundee Road, Suite 220
Northbrook, IL 60062
www.amprycp.com

www.rughookingmagazine.com

Printed in the United States of America

10 9 8 7 6 5 4 3 2 1

Cover design by Caroline M. Stover
Photographs by the author, unless otherwise indicated

Library of Congress Cataloging-in-Publication Data

Miller, Kristen L.
Introduction to rug hooking : a beginner's guide to tools, techniques, and
materials / Kristen L. Miller.—First edition.
    pages cm
  ISBN 978-1-881982-94-4
1. Rugs, Hooked. I. Title.
TT850.M515 2015
746.7'4--dc23
                          2014031480

TABLE OF CONTENTS

ACKNOWLEDGMENTS

Hydrangea, 27" x 43", #3- and 4-cut wool on rug warp. Designed by Jane McGown Flynn and hooked by Elaine Saxton, Howell, Michigan, 2010.
This is a beautiful and skillfully executed example of a realistic fine cut rug.

It is easy to teach someone a new skill when you are face to face and can give a hands-on demonstration to explain what you are doing. It's not so easy when you have to rely totally on the written word to get your point across. This is the monumental task I faced when I was asked to write this instructional book. How could I clearly put into words the actions and methods that are so easy to teach someone with my own two hands? Fortunately I still remembered the creative writing project I did in high school where I had to express only by written words the technique of how to tie a shoelace. Not an easy thing to do, but many years later, I drew from that experience to write this book. To that unknown English teacher (I am so sorry I have forgotten your name!) I give my deepest appreciation and gratitude.

There are many dear friends whose generosity and kindness helped this book become a reality. Thank you to Lisanne Miller, Elaine Saxton, and Keith Kemmer for donating your time and allowing me to borrow some of your rug hooking supplies. Thank you to my "Thursday Girls"—Sue Eaton, Sue McFall, Sheila Jolicoeur, and Pat Hagadon—for critiquing the completed hooked projects and for enthusiastically cheering me on. Thank you to my son, Kevin, for taking the time to shoot a few photographs when I was in a pinch.

Thank you to Barb Carroll, my very first teacher in color planning and textures, for your friendship, mentoring, and always being there when I needed sound advice.

Thank you to Deb Smith at Stackpole Books for all of your assistance and advice and believing that I could coax all the ideas out of my head and bring them to life on paper.

Most of all, my biggest and most heartfelt thanks goes to my husband, who endured the endless hours I spent writing at my computer or pulling up loops at my rug hooking frame, feverishly working toward my deadline. You became the chief cook and bottle washer, my errand boy, the dog walker and livestock feeder, the grocery shopper, photographer, consultant, and every other kind of helper who was needed to keep our lives on track while I was busy. I dragged you along while I dove deep into a life overflowing with wool and made you adopt it into your life as well. Thank you for sharing this crazy fun ride.

INTRODUCTION

I discovered rug hooking quite unexpectedly. I was sewing for a local clothing designer who created unique wool coats with intricately sewn designs cut out of hand-dyed wool fabrics. In her work studio, my sewing machine faced a long wall of wire shelving filled to the top with a rainbow of spot-dyed and mottled wool pieces. As I stared in awe at all of the luscious colors, I wondered where on earth would one find wool fabric that looked like that? I had never seen anything like it in fabric stores. "It's rug hooking wool," she said. A bell went off in my head. Rug hooking? I had to find out more about it!

I purchased two introductory rug hooking books and a copy of *Rug Hooking* magazine, and I sat down and read them from cover to cover. I scrutinized the photographs and read the instructions over and over. I called local quilt shops to find someone who taught rug hooking but most of them didn't even know what I was talking about. So I took a deep breath and jumped right in! I scrounged up a small piece of cheap burlap and hand cut some of my red dress-making wool flannel into ¼" strips. I drew out a heart, slipped my burlap into a flimsy embroidery hoop, and pulled up some loops. I told myself that I was going to sit in my chair until I could hook a complete outline around that heart! Every time I hooked a loop, the previous one would sink down into the burlap. My heart sank too. I was frustrated but wouldn't give up.

The rest, as they say, is history. Not only did I survive my first attempt, but the stars aligned, God smiled on me, and I fell head over heels in love with my new hobby. Not that I needed a new hobby, I told myself. I already knitted and sewed, and I was about to become the happy owner of three angora goats. Still, somehow, the thrill of using wool fabric, texture, and color completely stole my heart and all of my extra time. I was "hooked" on rug hooking!

Tropical Leopard, 28" x 37 ½", #8- and 8.5-cut wool and antique paisley on linen. Designed and hooked by Kris Miller, Howell, Michigan, 2006.
This is an example of a wide cut primitive rug with a naïve, folk art quality.

Welcome into the wonderful, colorful, creative world of rug hooking! You will begin to see color and design in an entirely different way. After I started to work on my first rug, I suddenly noticed the depth, values, and varieties of greens in the trees and foliage around me. I realized the sky was not just blue, but a whole symphony of colors that included pink, coral, and lavender. Even though I had worked with color my entire life, I had a fresh, new, and exciting perspective of how I could translate these beautiful hues into a wool rug. It is all about experiencing the wonderful texture of wool, and the calming rhythm of pulling up loops, while watching the color and shapes unfold right before your eyes into a charming design.

A hooked rug fits into any décor, whether it is modern, traditional, early American, primitive country, or shabby chic. The understated elegance and captivating designs will lure you into a quest for satisfying your own creativity. You will soon discover that you have become "hooked" on hooking rugs too!
—*Kris Miller*

1

What you need to know

CHAPTER 1

A Brief History of Rug Hooking

To appreciate rug hooking today, it is helpful to learn a little about its humble beginnings. There have been many differing opinions as to when and where it actually began.

Rug hooking most likely started sometime in the mid-1800s when jute was beginning to be mass-produced into burlap or hessian. Rug hooking was most prevalent in the New England states as well as the northeastern and maritime provinces of Canada. The hooked rug makers of that time were middle-to-lower-class families who could not afford the luxury of carpeting and needed something to brighten their hearth in summer and to keep their floors warm from the cold drafts in winter. Rug making was a pure and simple form of recycling: the jute from a feed or grain sack formed the rug's foundation, and old clothes that were too worn to pass down were cut into strips and worked through the weave of the sack with a hand-made tool to form a pile.

The whole process was a family affair. The husband often handcrafted a rug hook from a nail, a worn kitchen utensil, or an old key. He might have also crafted the wooden frame to hold the foundation tight. The children cut the clothing into narrow strips. Sometimes they sat beneath the frame to pass a new strip up to their mother who hooked the rug. Designs were often simple and naïve and not in proportion. A rug design might commemorate a special date or a scene from their everyday rural life. A horse or a dog might appear bigger than a house because it held greater importance to the rug maker. Geometric designs were popular because they were similar to quilting patterns and were easy to draw. A plate or a bowl served as a stencil for circles or curved arcs. These shapes could be repeated many times for a pleasing result. Other pattern inspirations came from crewel embroidery, seed catalogs, Turkish designs, or even fanciful patterns on china plates and cups.

Sailors also took up the craft of rug hooking to pass the dreary and lonely months at sea. Materials used were pieces of sisal roping that were untwisted and worked into a canvas foundation.

Three of the oldest rug hooks in this collection are fashioned from kitchen utensils. Can you spot them? The hook with the imprinted shield on its handle is believed to date back to the Civil War era. The top four hooks are from the author's collection. The bottom five hooks are from the collection of Elaine Saxton, Howell, Michigan.

Because the materials were often recycled, a rug might be hooked from a combination of fabrics such as cotton, dress silk, knit stockings, woolens, hand spun yarn, or untwined burlap. A newly hooked rug had a prominent spot in the parlor and as it wore, it was moved to the kitchen, and then to the back door, and eventually out to the woodpile where it kept the wood dry for the kitchen stove. Because the hooked rug was used in a utilitarian way and not necessarily viewed as a work of art, many of the early rugs have not survived for us to see today. The burlap broke apart or rotted and eventually the rugs became useless and were discarded. Surviving rugs from the 1800s are highly prized and sell for thousands of dollars at auction.

Edward Sands Frost is known to be the first commercial pattern maker for rug hooking. After serving briefly in the Civil War, he became a tin peddler by trade when his doctor advised him to find "outdoor work" due to his frail health. During the winter of 1868, his wife learned to hook rugs with the colorful rags he had collected. After watching her work, he decided that she needed a better rug hook and developed the bent hook, which is still a popular tool and used by many rug hookers today.

In testing his prototype hook, Frost became enamored with his new hobby and became a rug hooker himself. While working on his rug, he began to dream of better and prettier designs. His first sketched pattern was of a flower and scroll that he marked out on burlap, and he quickly received many orders for his designs from his neighbors. To save time and keep up with the growing demand, he created tin and zinc stencils from old wash boilers, cutting the floral, leaf, and scroll designs carefully into the metal. After printing them out with black ink, he put them

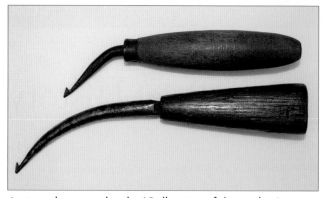

Antique bent rug hooks (Collection of the author)

on his peddler's cart and offered them for sale to the customers on his route.

Frost's customers developed an interest in patterns prestamped with colored ink since this took much of the guesswork out of color planning for eager rug makers in the 1870s. His color patterns became popular, and Frost sold his tin peddler business, opened a retail storefront in his town of Biddeford, Maine, and employed up to 10 people making patterns. His designs included floral bouquets, scrolls, and animals such as horses, lions, sheep, and ducks.

Due to failing health, he sold his pattern design business in 1876 and moved to California. While many other innovators and entrepreneurs helped shape the art and history of rug hooking, Edward Sands Frost created a lasting legacy for today's rug hookers, and his basic concepts have endured over two centuries. Many of his original designs continue to serve as inspiration for modern day rug makers.

Ducks (Pattern No. 17), 17" x 36¾"

This pattern was printed on burlap with the original Frost stencils at Greenfield Village and Henry Ford Museum, Dearborn, Michigan. From the author's collection.

Flowers and Leaves Antique Rug, 36½" x 21½", cotton, wool, and dress silk on burlap. Designer unknown.

This old rug is composed of old garments and backed with cotton ticking. The flowers, leaves, and diagonal lines are so random that it gives this rug a mysterious feeling.

Maple Leaves, 50" x 30", wool and cotton on burlap, circa early 1940s.

The pattern for this rug was most likely prestamped on the burlap and maybe a Bluenose Hooked Rug design. The rug maker used a flat wool braided finish to protect the edges. Despite the use of recycled fabrics, the maker has achieved wonderful shading in the leaves. Note how the striated hooked lines in the center add interest and energy to the entire rug.

CHAPTER 2

Tools of the Trade

HOOKS

The most important tool for rug hooking is the rug hook. The basic anatomy of a rug hook is a handle with a metal shaft and a barbed tip. Some hooks are made with crochet hooks and others are milled from steel or brass. The handles are most often wooden, but handles can also be metal, molded plastic, or polymer clay. Some hooks are very utilitarian while others are works of art.

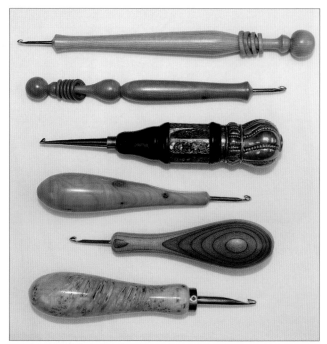

A variety of rug hooks.

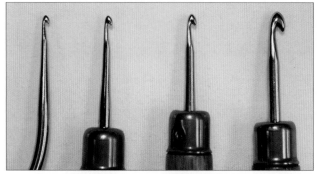

Samples of hook sizes. From left to right: fine, medium, coarse, primitive.

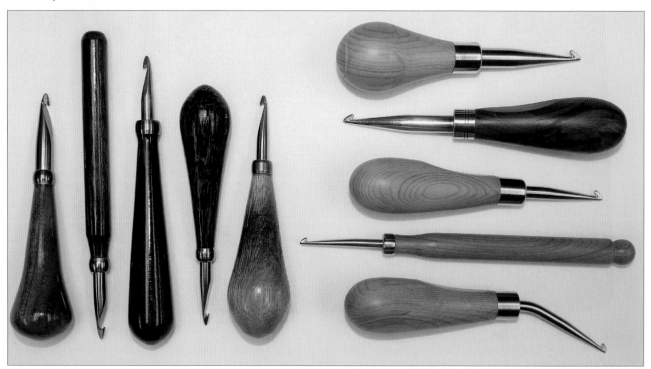

A collection of Ritchie hooks (left) and Hartman hooks (right).

6

Rug hooks come in many different styles. Some are long and thin: these are referred to as pencil hooks and are held just like you would hold a pencil. Others have chunky handles that nestle into the palm of your hand. Some rug hooks have a flat spot milled into the wooden handle to serve as a resting spot for your thumb or finger. I like these types of handles because the flat spot is an instant indicator that the barb of your hook is pointed toward the ceiling and therefore in the correct position to start hooking.

The rug hook's metal shaft and barb come in different sizes to handle different widths of cut wool strips. Most commonly, the hook sizes are fine, medium, coarse, and primitive. A fine hook most often handles #3- or 4-cut strips, while a medium hook is best for #5- or 6-cut strips. Coarse and primitive hooks work best for #6 cuts and wider. The Hartman hook and the Ritchie hook are both available in a variety of sizes; many rug hookers choose them because they have a wider shaft to accommodate larger cuts of wool. The thicker shaft helps separate the threads of the foundation cloth to enlarge the hole to make it easier to pull up a wide strip of wool. Some rug hooks are made with a metal shaft that is bent on an angle. This is a good choice for arthritic hands.

Choosing a rug hook is a personal choice, so it is best to try several styles and see which fits your hand and your style of hooking. You would not buy a pair of shoes without trying them on; it is the same when you purchase a rug hook. You want a nice fit that feels comfortable in your hand. Most rug hookers end up collecting a variety of rug hooks. Switching between two different hooks can ease stress and fatigue on your hands and wrists, and if you happen to lose one of your hooks, you will always have a backup.

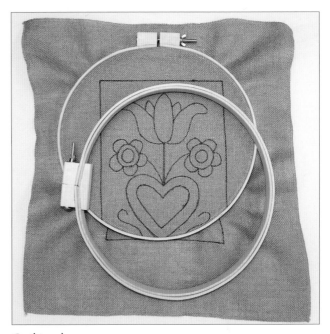

Quilting hoop

FRAMES

The second most important tool you need for rug hooking is something that will hold your foundation tight while you are pulling up your loops. An inexpensive choice for a beginner is a wooden quilting hoop. I recommend one that is 14" in diameter and at least 1" wide. Embroidery hoops are too thin and flexible to hold the weight of your hooked piece properly.

Rug hooking frames are usually square, rectangular, or round, made from wood, and have gripper strips fastened to the top. Gripper strips are small needle-like projections made of steel that are sharp and angled slightly outward. The foundation cloth is laid across the gripper strips and pulled tight for hooking. Your work can be moved and repositioned easily when you need to hook in a different spot.

Like hooks, rug hooking frames also come in many different styles. Some fit on a stand, some are made to

An example of a portable rug hooking frame. The Pittsburgh Crafting Frame can be folded up flat for storage or travel.

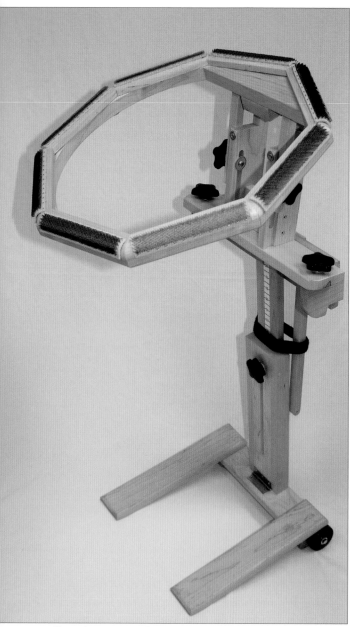

The Morton frame is an example of a simple, well-built lap frame.

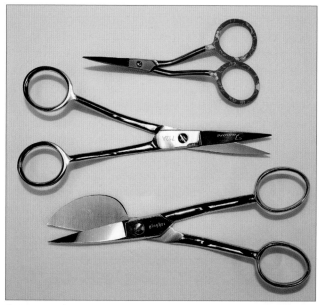

Scissor styles

A floor frame or a frame on a stand. The Needleworks stand adjusts in height and the octagonal frame conveniently rotates 360 degrees.

sit on your lap, and others fold up for travel. Finding a suitable rug hooking frame is a personal choice. Try out several frames to see which one works for you, or ask some of your rug hooking friends what frame they use or recommend.

Whether you use a hoop or a frame, always remove your work at the end of the day or when you are no longer hooking. Leaving the foundation cloth stretched tightly for an extended period of time may cause rippling or buckling, which will require extra steaming to get your finished project to lie flat later.

SCISSORS

You will be using your scissors constantly when you are rug hooking, so choose a pair of snips that are sharp and keep them close at hand. Regular dressmaker shears are too large. I prefer an appliqué scissor, either one with a bent handle or a "duck bill" blade. You can snip the ends closely without accidentally cutting into an adjacent loop.

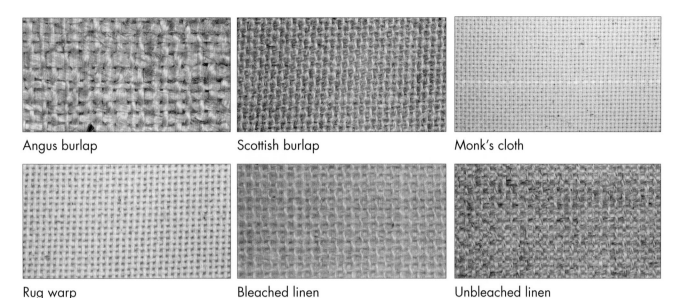

Angus burlap	Scottish burlap	Monk's cloth
Rug warp	Bleached linen	Unbleached linen

FOUNDATION CLOTH/BACKING

Burlap

Burlap is a loosely woven coarse fabric made from jute or sisal. It was the most commonly used rug hooking backing from the mid-1800s through the mid- to late-1900s. Early rug makers found burlap readily available as feed sacks and recycled it for rug making. It is available today in several different grades. Angus burlap is more coarsely woven with threads that may be more flat, uneven, and may contain slubs (a thick lump of soft fiber). Scottish burlap has an even weave with more round and refined threads.

Advantages: Burlap is inexpensive and readily obtained.

Disadvantages: Burlap can become brittle over time. Heat, moisture, continued wear, and improper storage will cause the fibers to break and disintegrate. It is also very linty and contains lots of wispy fibers that may show on the top of your rug. It can be rough on your hands and sometimes has a peculiar smell.

Monk's Cloth

Monk's cloth is woven from cotton fibers. It has an even weave containing two threads in both the warp and weft of the fabric. It has a creamy off-white color with distinctive white threads running through the fabric approximately 2" apart.

Advantages: Monk's cloth is relatively inexpensive. The cotton fibers are durable and will stand up to wear and tear for many years. It is soft on your hands. Its pliability makes it easy to use when sewing 3-dimensional pieces such as purses, toys, and so on.

Disadvantages: Monk's cloth can be stretchy and may be pulled out of shape, especially if the hooked loops are packed or the wool strips are ripped out too many times.

Rug Warp

Rug warp is made with a heavy string-like cotton yarn. It has an even weave and an off-white color.

Advantages: Rug warp is very durable and not as stretchy as monk's cloth. It is relatively inexpensive.

Disadvantages: It is heavier than linen or cotton, thus making larger rugs cumbersome to hook on a frame or hoop. It is often used for fine cut hooking. Pulling wide-cut strips through the weave could prove to be a bit more challenging.

Linen

Linen is woven from the fiber of the flax plant. The linen used in rug hooking is generally a coarse fabric with the opening between the threads wide enough to pull up wool strips. Primitive linen usually contains 12 threads per square inch. Linen woven for fine cut rug hooking contains a slightly tighter weave. Linen may be bleached (white) or unbleached (tan or beige).

Advantages: Linen will hold up to wear for many, many years. While its weave is similar to burlap, it is not as rough on your hands. It will not stretch like monk's cloth.

Disadvantages: Linen is the most expensive backing.

All foundation cloth will fray and unravel if the raw edges are not overcast or bound before hooking. You can choose one of several ways to do this. Finish the raw edge with a serger or sew close to the edge using a zigzag stitch on your sewing machine. Or simply wrap a piece of masking tape or duct tape around the raw edge.

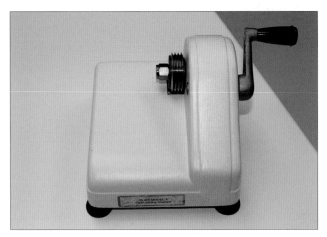
Bliss Model A

The Bolivar Standard Model contains three cutter heads that are not removable.

Fraser 500

The Bolivar Single Base Model V comes with one cutter head that can be removed and changed to a different size. It is lightweight and more portable than the Bolivar Standard Model.

MECHANICAL CUTTING MACHINES

Mechanical cutting machines are more commonly known as cutters, but they can also be called cloth slitting machines or strippers. They consist of a metal body with a hand crank and have a removable metal blade called a cutter head that will cut several strips of wool at the same time. A brand new cutter is expensive to purchase but is a joy to own. Wool strips are cut quickly and easily with just a turn of the crank. There are five major models to choose from: Bliss Model A, Fraser 500, Bee Line Art Tools (also known as the Townsend cutter), Bolivar Fabric Cutter, and Rigby.

Most of the cutting machines clamp securely to a table edge, except for the Bliss Model A, which has suction cup feet that stick to a smooth surface. Cutter heads are available in a wide variety of sizes from #2 to #12. Prices on new machines vary from model to model but your purchase will generally include one cutter head of your choice, a wrench, and basic instructions. If you are not able to purchase a new cutter, search E-Bay, Etsy, or Craig's List for used machines. Or you may find one at a garage sale, estate sale, or flea market. A friend of mine picked up a used Bliss cutter at a flea market for very little

Beeline Art Tools Fabric Cutter (also known as Townsend Fabric Cutter)

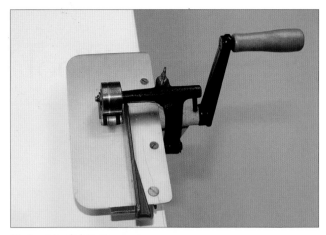

Rigby Model D Cutter

Cutter heads for the Bliss Model A and Fraser 500 (left) and cutter head "cassettes" for the Bee Line Art Tools Fabric Cutter (right).

money because the vendor thought it was an old pasta maker!

After hooking a few projects, you will probably realize that it is most convenient to have more than one size cutter head on hand. I recommend buying at least a #6 and #8 since these sizes seem to be the most versatile for a beginner.

Keep your cutter free of dust and wool lint, which builds up quickly after a session of cutting wool strips. The lint gets packed tightly into small areas so use a small brush or canned air to dislodge the clumps of dust from in between the cutter head and the table of

the machine. Refer to the instructions that came with your cutter to see if it needs a drop of oil occasionally. Routine cleaning and maintenance will keep your machine cutting smoothly for many years. If, for some reason, your machine needs to be fixed, contact the original manufacturer for expert repair service or additional replacement parts.

CHAPTER 3

Wool Wisdom

Recycled wool

The earliest hooked rugs were made from all types of recycled fabrics such as cotton, silk, wool, stockings, or even sisal fiber. Today's hooked rugs are predominately hooked with 100% wool. Wool is resilient, resists dirt, and holds up under everyday wear and tear. It springs back when crushed and has a wonderful loft and softness that lends itself very well to the beautiful art of rug making.

You can recycle wool from apparel in your closet that you no longer wear, old garments donated by generous friends, or purchased clothing from a thrift shop. Be sure to wash them as soon as they come into your house. Used clothing is often dirty from wear or leftover dry cleaning fluids, and you do not want to bring any unwanted pests, such as moths, into your home. Deconstructing the garments outside will cut down on lint, dirt, and any hidden bugs entering your house too. Remove any linings before washing the garment. The lining will bleed its color into the wash

water, and often it will shrink more than the wool, causing everything to become a bunched-up mess in the washing machine.

After the garment is washed and dried, use a seam ripper to open up all seams and hems. Cut off the

Textured wool

A sampling of wool flannel suitable for fine-cut hooking. From left to right: dip-dyed wool, graduated color swatches, spot-dyed wool.

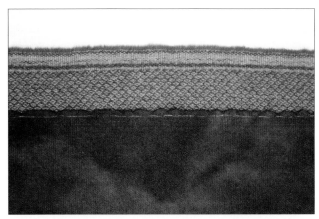

A flat woven band (top) and a distinct white thread indicate the selvedge edge of these two wool pieces.

waistbands, cuffs, collars, plackets, and any parts that have fused interfacing, which is nearly impossible to remove. Garments that yield the most wool are pleated kilts, skirts, and pants. Look for old woolen scarves, army blankets, military uniforms, and damaged paisley shawls. Shirts, blazers, and suit jackets will yield smaller amounts of usable wool. Garments that have 100% wool on the label are the most desirable. Blends can be used, but do not buy any wool combined with polyester or other wool blends that have less than 85% wool. These fabrics will not felt thick enough to create usable hooking material nor will they dye well. Suitable wool fabrics include tweeds, herringbones, camel, wool flannel, heathers, bouclés, checks, and plaids. Don't overlook woolens that have tears, worn spots, or moth holes; these bad spots can be cut around and the rest of the wool will still be usable. Unsuitable fabrics such as serge, gabardine, some twill weave, and worsted suiting material have a flat, thin feel and are difficult to hook. Don't waste your money on them.

If you find a mystery fabric of unknown origin, you can do a simple test to see if it is 100% wool. Snip off about a 1" piece of the mystery fabric and place it in a glass jar. Pour a couple of inches of household beach into the jar so that it covers the snippet of fabric. Put a lid on the jar and allow the fabric to sit overnight. If the fabric is 100% wool, the bleach will have eaten it away and nothing will remain in the jar except for the bleach. If there are other fibers that have been blended with the wool, they will remain as little threads in the solution.

Many rug hookers buy new wool by the yard in fabric stores or order wool by mail. There are several good sources for purchasing wool by mail (*see Resources*). Hook-ins, rug camps, online rug hooking suppliers, and fiber festivals are also good places to look for woolen materials. You will often find that the wool purchased at these venues is already washed or overdyed and ready to cut and hook right away.

The term *textured wool* is applied to wool that has a distinctive weave to it, such as plaids, herringbones, checks, stripes, heathers, bouclés, and tweeds. Because of its unique weave, textured wool may leave some loose threads on the surface of your work when hooking. Simply trim these threads off as you are working and do not worry about them. Textured wool is perfect for wide-cut hooking, and if you are careful, it can be used in fine-cut hooking too.

Wool flannel usually has a tighter and more even weave, which is suitable for fine-cut hooking. Look for it in a variety of solid colors or dyed into a myriad of mottled shades and graduated color swatches.

You must always wash your wool before you hook it. Washing will felt the wool, making it a little thicker and softer to work with. You do not, however, want to felt it so much that it is thick like a blanket, which would make it hard to pull up through your backing material. Place your wool in the washing machine with a liquid detergent such as Tide, Gain, or Ivory, and fill the machine with cool to lukewarm water. Never use bleach or products that contain bleach. Wash the wool with a gentle cycle, rinse it in cold water, and let the washer spin until all the water is gone. Remove the wool from the washer, and place it in a dryer set on warm. Use an old clean towel or dryer ball, which will help fluff out the wool so it will dry evenly. Your wool should come out soft and fluffy. If the wool still feels thin after it has been washed, you can try washing it again. Proceed with caution, however, because once wool is felted too thickly, you cannot reverse the process.

Wool must always be cut on the straight of the weave of the fabric for rug hooking. If the cut is on the bias, the wool strip will shred and fall apart. Find the selvedge edge of the fabric. The selvedge edge is usually tightly woven and may have a small white or colored cotton or nylon thread running along the outer edge.

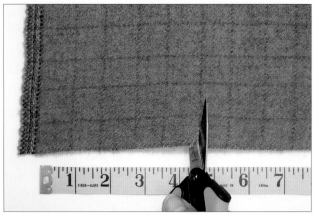

1. Measure over 4" to 5" from the selvedge, and make a small snip with your scissors.

2. Grasp the wool on either side of the snip with your hands, and rip off the piece. When you rip the wool in this manner, you will always be on the straight of the grain of the fabric. It will be much more accurate than if you tried to cut straight with a pair of scissors.

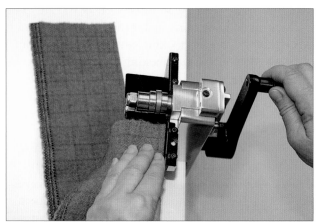

3. Take the ripped piece of wool to the cutter. Turn the crank with your right hand and run the piece of wool through the blades by carefully holding it straight and guiding it with your left hand.

4. Don't try to cut anything larger than a 4" to 5" piece of wool at one time. You will risk the chance of cutting unevenly or cutting off-grain. After you make your first pass through the cutter, flip the piece of wool over and begin to cut from the other end.

Flipping your wool from end to end will help to keep your strips straight and even. Avoid the temptation to cut all of your wool at one time. Cut only as much as you need for one sitting at your frame.

The length of your strip is a personal decision, but I like to hook with strips that are between 14" and 32" long. Hooking with anything shorter than 12" is not efficient — the wool strip will not go very far. Strips that are longer than 32" become a nuisance, and you risk accidentally pulling them out if they become entangled underneath your frame or if you unknowingly sit on them as you are hooking.

Strip sizes left to right: #3 ($^3/_{32}$"), #4 ($^1/_8$"), #5 ($^5/_{32}$"), #6 ($^6/_{32}$"), #7 ($^7/_{32}$"), #8 ($^1/_4$"). Note: These strips were cut on a Beeline Art Tools Fabric Cutter.

Strip sizes left to right: #8.5 ($^5/_{16}$"), #9 ($^3/_8$"), #10 ($^1/_2$"), #11 ($^3/_4$"), #12 (1"). Note: these strips were cut on a Beeline Art Tools Fabric Cutter.

STRIP SIZES

In the rug hooking world, the width of a cut strip is based on $^1/_{32}$". Therefore, a #4 strip is really $^4/_{32}$", or $^1/_8$". A #8 strip is $^8/_{32}$" or $^1/_4$". Cutter heads are available in sizes #2 through #12 and sometimes wider, depending on the manufacturer.

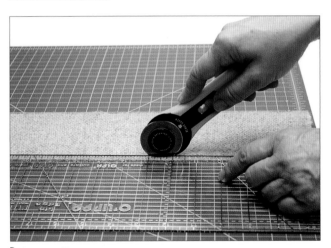

Rotary cutter

Hand cutter

CUTTING WITH A ROTARY CUTTER

If you are cutting with a rotary cutter and self-healing mat, use a clear ruler with $^1/_4$" markings. Carefully line up the ripped edge with the $^1/_4$" mark on the ruler and use the rotary cutter to cut a strip. It is important to only cut 3" to 4" at a time, and then start again with another freshly torn piece of wool. That way, you will be keeping your strips as straight as possible with every new tear.

HAND CUTTING WOOL

Perhaps you don't have access to a cutting machine or a rotary cutter, or maybe you want an antique look for your rug. Consider hand cutting your wool strips. The best results will come from using 100% wool that is tightly woven. Snip and tear a $^1/_2$" piece of wool. Hold the wool tightly between your fingers with one hand, and carefully cut directly down the center of the torn strip with the other hand. Each resulting strip will be $^1/_4$" wide and consist of a straight cut side and a fuzzy torn side which will give your rug a wonderful vintage look.

Fold wool to estimate quantity needed.

Bundle small pieces and tie them with a strip of wool.

Store wool strips in plastic bags.

Organize large pieces on shelves.

ESTIMATING WOOL QUANTITIES

Estimating the quantity of wool you need is not an exact science. You must consider the height and spacing of your loops. If you pull your loops very high or you pack your loops, you will need more wool than someone who does not. If you are hooking your strips ¼" high and not packing your loops, you will generally require 4 to 5 times the amount of wool for the area that needs to be hooked. The best way to do this is to fold a piece of wool four or five times and place it over the area that needs to be hooked. If it covers the area comfortably, then it should be enough. If there is too little or too much wool, refold the wool so that the four or five layers fit better. It is always advisable to overestimate your wool quantity than to run short, so always add some extra to your estimated amount. Rug hookers who pull up their wool higher or who pack their loops should estimate at least 5 to 6 times the amount of wool needed for a specific area.

Wool colors and textures may only be available for a short amount of time and then they may disappear. When purchasing wool for a project, always buy a little more than you think you will need. You will avoid the disappointment and frustration of running out and trying to hunt it down at a later time.

When buying wool to supplement my stash, I look for stripes and unusual textures. Stripes offer multiple colors in just one piece, and unusual woven textures add a special spark and dimension to your hooked rug.

STORING WOOL

Many options are available for storing wool. You can temporarily store your freshly cut wool strips in plastic zipper-top bags, sorted according to color. This makes your current hooking project more organized and portable, and will keep the wool dust down to a minimum in your work area.

Once recycled wool garments are washed and deconstructed, the pieces can be stacked and rolled up together jelly-roll style. Fasten the whole bundle together with a discarded waistband or an extra strip of wool.

Quarter yard or half yard pieces of wool look gorgeous when they are folded and organized according to color on open shelving. Antique cupboards or wire cube shelving units (found at department or home improvement stores) are other wonderful possibilities to keep your wool in view for inspiration and color planning. Store larger quantities of wool yardage in storage bins in a closet or under a bed. Whatever

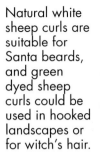

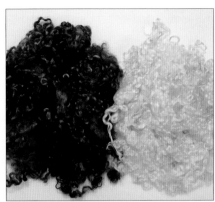

Natural white sheep curls are suitable for Santa beards, and green dyed sheep curls could be used in hooked landscapes or for witch's hair.

A variety of beautiful fabric pieces from antique paisley shawls.

Novelty yarns

Roving is a soft loose "rope" of unspun wool fiber. Clockwise from top: Brown alpaca and mohair blend, pure white alpaca, gray Romney wool and mohair blend.

method you choose to store your wool, make sure it is in a cool, dry place away from direct sunlight. Tuck moth-repelling cedar or lavender sachets in between the layers of wool to keep unwanted pests away.

ALTERNATIVE RUG HOOKING MATERIALS

While wool is the fabric of choice in today's hooked rugs, other alternative materials can enhance your design. Give yourself permission to experiment, play, and have fun. You are only limited by your imagination.

Hooking strips of vintage paisley into select accent spots in your rug will give your work an antique feel and a soft glow that cannot be reproduced by any fabric made today. When cutting paisley, always cut in the direction the long threads run along the back of the fabric and cut the strips at least one size bigger than the rest of the strips in your rug. For best results, cut it no less than a #8 cut. Folding a cut strip of paisley in half will give you a better option for a smaller hooking width. Paisley is expensive, so only cut a few strips at a time to avoid waste. Paisley also frays easily, so hook it carefully and trim away any

stray threads that may appear on the top of your work.

Yarn is another great way to enhance your rug. The possibilities are endless. Use yarn to supplement texture in landscapes, animals, Halloween creatures, bird feathers, hair, flowers. . . . The list goes on and on. Yarn composed with any type of fiber content can be mixed with rug hooking. If the yarn is thick, it can be pulled up just like a wool strip, and if it is thin, it can be used as an accent and pulled up through the spaces in between rows of hooked loops. I love the look of novelty yarns such as eyelash yarn, glitter yarns, and yarns with lumps and bumps.

Sheep curls and roving are easy to hook. Natural white can be used in Santa beards, sheep, clouds, and rabbit tails. Dyed roving and sheep curls are perfect for hair, flowers, landscapes, and animals. You can purchase both sheep curls and roving at sheep and wool festivals and fiber shows.

Cotton homespun and other types of cotton cloth may be cut or torn into strips and used in rug hooking. Look for cotton that is the same color on both sides for best results. I recommend using cotton fabric

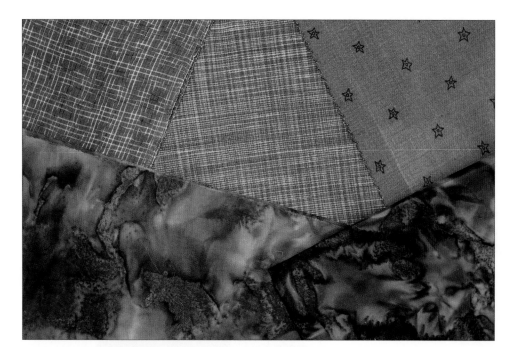

Cotton and homespuns

Nylon stockings and children's tights

Ribbon from recycled fabric

as an accent area combined with your wool strips. Cotton does not have the resiliency and loft of wool and tends to mat down and retain dirt easier.

Other alternative materials include knit sweaters and hosiery (such as nylon stockings and tights). Sweaters and hosiery should be hand cut across the knit, and the strips should be cut larger than the actual size you want to hook. Hold the ends of the strip in each hand and pull gently. The cut ends will roll inward forming a tube and the strip will be reduced in

size, ready for hooking. Nylon stockings can be dyed in many beautiful colors.

Ribbon is wonderful embellishment in your hooked rugs. Sari ribbon and reclaimed chiffon ribbon are favorite choices for rug hooking. They are made from recycled silk sari garments and remnant fabrics from India and Nepal. Hook ribbon just as you would hook a wool strip. You will discover that it adds extra dimension, color, and whimsy.

CHAPTER 4

How to Hook

You may want to use a scrap piece of foundation cloth to practice your hooking technique until you feel ready to start working on your first project. If you have a pattern already, you can practice on the extra fabric of the outside margins until you feel confident to start working on the actual design.

Sit in a comfortable chair with good lighting. Your back should be straight and your feet should be flat on the floor. Don't hunch over your frame. Have a convenient spot nearby to keep your hook, extra wool strips, and scissors. Keep a small container close by so you can neatly discard your scraps and snipped off ends.

How to Pull Up Loops

1. Stretch your foundation cloth over the gripper strips of your rug hooking frame.

2. With your hands, pull the edges evenly all the way around so the grain of the foundation cloth is fairly straight and the design is not wavy or distorted. You want the stretched cloth to be firm and as taut as possible. I like to imagine that I can bounce a quarter off of my tightened foundation cloth.

3. If you are using a quilting hoop, center the design on the foundation cloth on the inner hoop and place the outer hoop over the foundation cloth. As you tighten the screw on the outer hoop, adjust the foundation cloth so that it becomes taut and the grain of the fabric is fairly even.

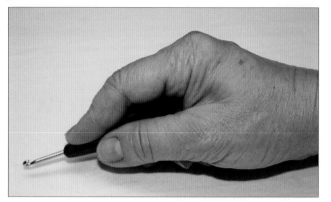

4. There is no right or wrong way to hold your hook. It must be comfortable for you and not bother your hand, wrist, or elbow. Many people hold their hook like a pencil, while others hold their hook with the handle nestled inside their palm. Experiment to see which way is more comfortable for your hand.

Hold the hook with the barb pointed up toward the ceiling. If there is a flat spot on the handle of your hook, rest your thumb or finger in this area. This flat spot serves as an easy reference because it is located in the position to assure the barb of the hook points up.

5. Cut a piece of wool into ¼" (#8) strips. Grasp a wool strip in your left hand (if you are left-handed, hold it in your right hand). Slip the strip between your index finger and your middle finger and again between your thumb and your ring finger. Hold the wool strip firmly but in such a way that it can slide through your fingers easily. If it is more comfortable, you can hold the wool strip so that it passes just between your thumb and forefinger.

6. Place your hand holding the wool strip underneath the foundation cloth that is stretched tight over your frame or hoop. Make sure your fingers are resting right up against the foundation cloth and you are holding the wool strip loosely but securely. Your fingers should be placed directly underneath where you want to hook.

7. On the right side of your work, the right hand (or left hand, if you are left-handed) should be holding the rug hook with the barb pointed up toward the ceiling. Insert the hook into a hole in the foundation cloth.

8. Keep the shaft of the hook at approximately a 45-degree angle (not straight up and down and not horizontal), and as it passes through the foundation cloth, let it slip between your fingers holding the wool strip underneath. Catch the width of the wool strip with the barb of the hook.

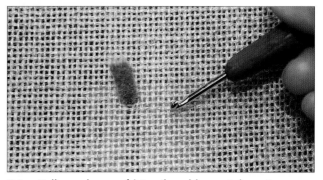

9. Pull up the end to the top of your foundation cloth.

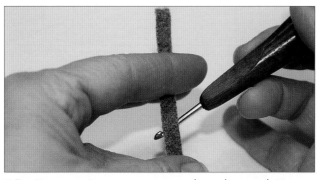

10. Do not twist, wrap, or try to knot the wool. You are merely scooping up the strip of wool and bringing the end up to the surface.

This is how your hands and rug hook should be positioned if you were to view them without the obstruction of the foundation cloth. Note that the hook is at a 45-degree angle and the barb is pointed up toward the ceiling and ready to scoop up the strip of wool from between the fingers. (Finger position is exaggerated to show detail.)

11. Pull up about a ¹/₂" tail and leave it hanging on the right side.

12. Now push your hook down into the next hole, slide the hook between your fingers beneath the foundation cloth and underneath the wool strip you are holding, and pull up a loop.

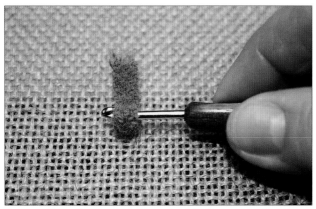

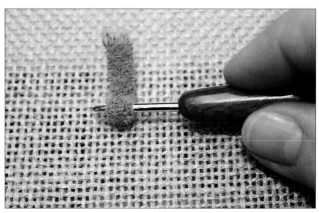

13. Pull the loop up at least 1/4" high. You will notice that because the barb is still pointed up toward the ceiling, the barb is catching on the edge of the strip, thus preventing you from slipping the hook out of the loop easily.

14. Gently rotate your hook so that the barb is now pointing downward toward the floor.

15. If desired, you can pull down very slightly on the wool strip with your left hand to even out the height of your loop. Slip your hook out of the loop you have just formed. You have just created your first loop!

16. For the next loop, skip a hole and poke your hook down into the second hole in your foundation cloth.

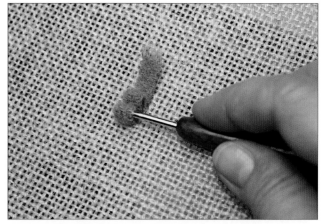

17. Again, slip the hook between your fingers to scoop up the wool strip, pull a loop to the top of your work, rotate your hook so that the barb is pointing downward, adjust the height of the loop if necessary, and remove your hook. Continue this process of skipping every other hole and hook a straight line of loops until you get to the end of your wool strip.

18. When your strip of wool becomes too short to hook any more loops, insert your hook in the next hole. Do not skip a hole this time. Pull the end of the wool strip to the top of your work, leaving about a ½" tail.

19. Hold a new wool strip in your left hand under your foundation cloth. Insert your hook in the same hole where the previous strip ended and pull up the end of the new strip. You will have two ends coming up in the same hole, each protruding about ½".

20. Continue to hook by pulling up a loop in the very next hole.

21. Then continue to skip every other hole while you are pulling up the remaining loops.

22. After you get a few loops hooked, go back and trim the ends. Cut them off even with the rest of your loops. Once you get enough hooked in, these cut ends will not show.

23. Remember that all of your ends should come to the top of your work; never leave them on the bottom. You are locking the ends in place when you hook two ends in the same hole. The loops on either side of the two ends will help hold them in place.

Most rug hookers hook their strips from right to left or from top to bottom (hooking the row toward them). If you are left-handed, you will find it easier to hook from left to right. Feel free to turn your rug hooking frame or hoop in any direction you wish as you are hooking. This makes it easier to see where you are going and prevents awkward positions that could put a strain on your arm, wrist, or shoulder.

TROUBLESHOOTING

Now that you have hooked a few strips, stop to examine your work.

Make sure you are pulling your loops high enough. If the loops are pulled up too low, you may have trouble getting your hook out of the newly formed loop. The general rule is that the loops should be as high as your strip is wide. An easy way to test for this is to take an extra strip and set it on its side right next to the row you have just hooked. Your loops should be as tall as the strip. Keep practicing so that all your loops are at a relatively even height. This may take some patience at first. Remember, the world will not end if they are a little bit uneven! You will soon find your rhythm and the height that is normal for you.

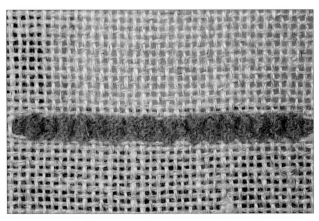

Look carefully at the back. Make sure that all the loops are being pulled to the top of your work and that you have no lumps or accidental loops left on the back. You want the bottom of your work to be as flat and smooth as possible to avoid excessive wear and possible damage to the wool strips later.

Check for twisted loops. If your loops are coming up twisted, you are most likely not keeping your fingers pressed right up against the backing material while you are holding your wool strip underneath your work. When your fingers are held away from the backing, you will hunt and dig with your hook to find the strip of wool, thus causing the twist. Simply pull out the twisted stitch, readjust the position of your hand underneath the foundation cloth, and pull up the loop again.

Watch for "sinking" loops. You may find that you are pulling out the previous loop as you are hooking, or the previous loop is sinking down lower while you are pulling up the next loop. You can conquer this problem by simply pulling your current loop back at an angle toward the previous loop you have just hooked. It will be impossible for the previous loops to sink when you use this technique.

MORE BASIC KNOWLEDGE

Skipping holes. You should never hook in every single hole of your backing. Doing so will pack your work so tightly that the rug would never lie flat or have a soft, supple feel. It is acceptable to skip every other hole, or every second hole, when hooking primitive or wide cut rugs. For fine cut rugs, you would hook in every hole for three or four loops and then skip one hole.

Starting a new color. When you want to start a new color, simply bring the end of your current strip up to the top of your work and snip it off, leaving a ¹/₂" tail. Start the strip of new color by pulling its end up in the same hole where the previous strip ended. Never cross your strips underneath your work to hook in a new spot! This bad habit causes little floats that will leave a lump on the bottom of your work. The lumps will wear out quickly on the floor and, if they accidentally catch on something, will cause your hooked loops to be pulled out.

Starting a new row. When hooking a new row, make sure the shoulders of the loops are touching but not hugging each other. The rows should be spaced close enough so that you cannot see the backing in between the rows but not so close that the loops are pushing in on each other. The loops should look round and plump and not crushed, angled, or V-shaped. Measure over about two or three threads in the foundation for a wide cut rug, and one or two

Shoulders touching

Hook rows 2–3 threads over from the previous row

Staggered rows

threads for a fine cut rug. Generally, the wider the strip, the more threads you will have to count over to place the next row. As you begin to hook more rows, stagger your cut ends so they do not line up in the same spot from row to row. Your eye will automatically see these areas otherwise. If you find that the cut ends keep occurring in the same spot, purposely end the strip and start a new one before you reach that area.

As a beginner, you will be acutely aware that you have to count holes, spaces, and threads. Once you become comfortable with your own rhythm, you will find that you no longer need to count, and the spacing will become automatic.

Fixing mistakes. If you make a mistake or discover that you do not like a color as you are hooking, rip out the offending loops and start again. Pull down gently on the wool strip from the bottom of your work until it comes loose from the foundation. You can usually use this wool strip again despite the fact that it looks crimped or has a few loose threads.

Removing your work from a hoop or frame. To take your hooked project out of a quilting hoop, loosen the wing nut at the top and pull open the outer ring to release the foundation cloth. To remove your rug from a rug hooking frame with gripper strips, first grasp the closest edge of the foundation cloth

Removing work from a rug hooking frame

TIPS FOR NEW RUG HOOKERS

1. Never use pure solid black or pure solid white wool in your hooking project. The colors are too harsh by themselves and will stand out like a beacon in your rug.

2. It is perfectly acceptable to mix different sizes of cut strips in your rug.

3. Feel free to turn your frame in any direction when you are hooking.

4. Always remove your backing from your frame overnight or when you will not be hooking for an extended period of time.

5. The more you practice, the better your rug hooking will become. Try to rug hook every day, even if it's only for a half hour. I often hook while watching the evening news. Listen to music or a book on tape. Keep your frame, wool strips, and hook close to your favorite chair so it is easy to steal a few minutes to hook.

6. Embrace your individuality. Try not to compare your hooking style to someone else's. We all have our unique ways of doing things. Your hooking style is like your thumbprint. Over time, others will recognize and appreciate it.

7. Join a local rug hooking group or find someone in your area to hook with. Not only will you enjoy the camaraderie of like-minded people, but it is a great time to exchange ideas and learn new techniques.

8. Enjoy your new hobby. Let the stress of the day slip away, relax, and have fun!

with one hand. Slowly pull this edge straight out toward you until the foundation begins to loosen. Turn your frame and repeat this step on an adjacent side. Once you feel the foundation loosen from the gripper strips on both sides, gently lift the entire piece off of the frame. By tugging on your rug without loosening it first, you run the risk of pulling out some of the hooked loops that are still attached to the needles of the gripper strips.

Dealing with worms. After hooking a few projects, you will have accumulated a quantity of leftover wool strips, often called worms or noodles. In true pioneer spirit, a rug hooker rarely discards any bits and pieces of material that might be useful in another project at a different time. Store your leftover strips in a bin or container, sorted by color so they can be quickly accessed if you need just a little piece. I do not save any scraps or strips that are less than 3" because they are generally too short to work with.

CHAPTER 5

How to Draw a Pattern

A large and widely varied selection of rug hooking patterns are commercially available through pattern designers and rug hooking businesses. These patterns are already drawn out on the backing of your choice and are ready to hook. However, designing and drawing a pattern yourself doesn't have to be intimidating if you take your time and follow a few important steps.

Design inspirations are everywhere. Children's drawings, your own doodles, and personal photographs are just a few design possibilities. Think of memorializing a special event, honoring a beloved pet, or celebrating your favorite holiday. Look for free-use clip art books at your local bookstore or library. Some craft books and magazines specifically publish free patterns to enlarge and hook for your own personal use.

Once you have chosen a design or sketched out your own, you may need to enlarge it to the correct size. Specialized computer software programs are geared toward enlarging designs so you can print them out on your printer at home. You may find that once the design is printed, you will have to tape several pieces of paper together in order to get the

Darken those lines with a permanent marker.

correct size for the entire pattern. An easier option is to take your drawn design to an office supply store and have it enlarged for a nominal charge.

Once the design is the correct size, you will need to determine the size to cut the foundation cloth. Use the dimensions of your pattern and add an extra margin of at least 4 inches all the way around so that it will fit easily onto your frame or hoop. For instance, a pattern design that measures 12" x 16" would require a piece of foundation cloth that measures at least 20" x 24". The foundation cloth will easily unravel, so it is important to serge, zigzag stitch, or wrap your raw edges with duct tape or masking tape before transferring your design.

When drawing your design directly on the backing, always use a black waterproof or permanent marker such as Sharpie or Rub-A-Dub.

It is extremely important that your pattern is drawn on the straight of the grain of the foundation cloth. I always draw my outside border lines first. If you are drawing straight lines, here is a clever trick to get them straight on the grain. Use a sharp pencil and place the tip in between two threads in the foundation cloth. This is called the *ditch*. Hold the pencil at a 45-degree angle and carefully drag the pencil tip along the ditch. After you establish your border lines with the pencil, you should retrace them with a fresh, sharp Sharpie marker. You can draw the rest of the design elements on the foundation cloth once the border lines are marked.

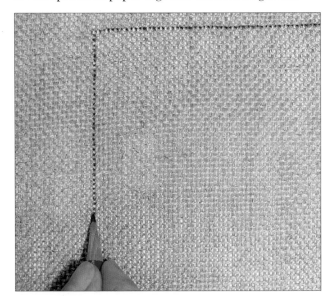
Draw border lines in the "ditch."

Line up red dot tracer on the pattern.

There are several ways to transfer the design to your backing. Using a light table is the easiest method. You can improvise by using a glasstop table and putting a small lamp underneath it. On a sunny day, you can tape your paper pattern to a window and then tape your foundation cloth on top of that. Or use bridal netting, red dot tracer, or fiberglass screening material found at your local hardware store.

Red dot tracer is a nonwoven lightweight material similar to interfacing. Small red dots are marked at 1" intervals throughout the material. Lay the red dot tracer over your paper pattern. Line up the red dots so that they follow the straight lines of your outside border. Use dressmaker weights or pin the red dot tracer to your paper to keep it from shifting while you are drawing. With a waterproof marker, carefully trace over your entire paper design.

Measure and draw the outside border lines on your foundation cloth with the marker. Remember to measure in at least 4" from the raw edge. Now lay the red dot tracer on top of your foundation cloth. Center the design by matching the drawn border lines on both the foundation cloth and red dot tracer. Pin or affix it in place and carefully retrace the design. Firmly press the marker tip into the red dot tracer to get a dark line. Once you are done, remove the red dot tracer and redraw over any faint lines or skipped spots. If you are using bridal netting or screening material, follow this same process.

If you purchase a commercial pattern that is not on

Trace the pattern lines.

Place the red dot tracer on the foundation and retrace the design.

Connect the dots.

the straight of the grain of the foundation cloth, you should first try to return it for a refund or exchange it for a new pattern. If that is not possible, you will have to square it up yourself. Redraw the lines by dragging your marker in the ditch on the straight of the grain. Draw as close to the original lines as you possibly can but make them straight. You may have to adjust the rest of the design, depending on how off kilter the original lines were drawn. Use a permanent marker in a different color (such as blue) so that you will not confuse your new marks with the original markings.

A WORD ABOUT COPYRIGHT

Copyright is the legal protection of someone's intellectual rights. Included in this law are literary, musical and dramatic works, pictorial, graphic and sculptural works, sound recordings, motion pictures, and architectural works. Copyright is indicated by the symbol ©. Most images you see on the Internet are protected by copyright, even if credit is not specifically given to the artist or creator.

Never copy someone else's designs or artwork without written permission from the artist. This includes retracing a pattern you have already purchased to make more than one copy of the same pattern, either to share with a friend or to duplicate it for your own use. If you need two patterns, you must buy two patterns.

Some people think it's permissible to copy a design for their own use because it's only meant to be displayed in their own house and they are not going to resell it. This is not only a copyright violation but is actually considered stealing. The common misconception of changing a design "seven times" or altering it "fifty percent" is also not acceptable and is unlawful.

Stars, hearts, diamonds, and other simple geometric shapes are considered common design elements that are not copyrightable and are free for anyone to use. However, once you begin to place these shapes into distinct arrangement, a unique design begins to form and the work becomes copyrightable and protected by law.

Copyright laws cover the rights of an artist for their lifetime plus 70 years. Any design prior to 1923 is deemed to be in the public domain and is open to use. When in doubt, the best advice is to contact the copyright owner and ask for permission to use his or her artwork. To protect yourself, obtain a written consent. If the artist does not respond, cannot be reached, or says no to your request, just move on and choose a different design.

Resist the temptation to copy, whatever the reason may be!

More information about copyright can be found on the US Copyright Office's website, *www.copyright.gov.*

CHAPTER 6

Finishing a Hooked Rug

Y ou've pulled up your last loop and your hooking is completed. Now what should you do? The final steps of finishing your project are a critical part of creating a beautiful rug. A hooked rug without a good finish is like baking a cake and serving it to your guests without the frosting. It's not the "whole package" until you perform the last few important steps.

Mark them with toothpicks.

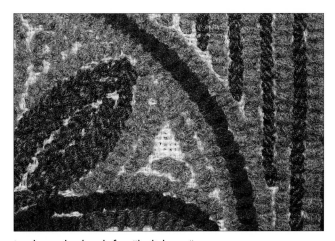

Look on the back for "holidays."

HOLIDAYS

Remove the rug from your frame and check for holidays. A *holiday* is a funny expression that means that there was a forgotten spot on your rug where no loops were hooked. Most of the time, you won't be able to see holidays unless you flip your rug over to the back and examine your hooking. It is normal to have small spaces on the back of your rug where the foundation cloth is showing between your rows of hooking. If you did not have these spaces, the rug would be hooked too tight, making it stiff and inflexible. A holiday is larger and more noticeable than those normal empty spaces.

If a holiday is left unhooked, dirt could work its way down to the foundation cloth causing that spot in the rug to wear out prematurely. Additionally, the loops in this skipped area are more likely to be

Fill them from the front by adding loops.

snagged and pulled out. You can mark a holiday by temporarily sticking a round toothpick through the back of your foundation cloth. Then, when you look at the right side of your work, you will easily find them. Use matching wool strips and fill in the holidays from the front.

Carefully trim off any stray threads that may be popping up on the front of your work or hanging from the back. Examine your rug for any other final adjustments.

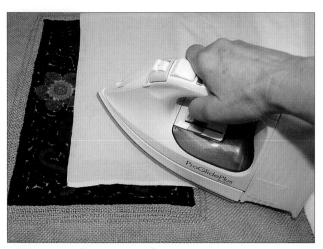
Steam press the wrong side.

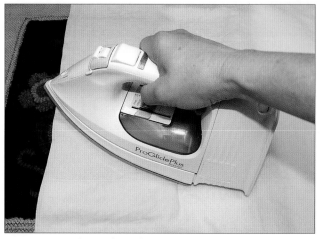
Steam press the right side.

STEAMING/PRESSING

Perhaps your hooked edges have curled under a little bit or the circular areas have heaved up and look like domes, or your rug surface may look slightly rippled or wavy. Steaming your rug is the magic that will correct all these problems. Steaming not only flattens your rug and lessens the unevenness, it will make your hooking look neater and feel more soft and supple.

Find a place that is large enough to accommodate your entire rug so that it lies flat. Do not try to steam on an ironing board where the rug edges will be hanging off the sides. Do not use a table that has a varnished surface or any other surface that would be ruined by moisture. Use a table or countertop that is water and heat resistant. I spread everything out on the linoleum tile floor in my studio.

Fill your steam iron with water, plug it in, and set the temperature to the wool setting. While the iron is heating up, lay down a few layers of clean old towels or wool blankets (found at thrift shops). The layers will create a soft, firm, base that will help pull the steam completely through your rug. Lay your hooked rug face down on top of these layers.

I recommend using a clean old cotton dishtowel as a press cloth. Take the press cloth to the sink and get it thoroughly wet. Wring out some of the excess water so it is not drippy and lay it out flat, directly on top of your rug. Use the steam setting on your iron and press the iron against the wet press cloth in a firm down-ward motion. Do not slide the iron as if you were ironing a shirt. Push it firmly into the press cloth for a few seconds, lift it up, and move to another area.

Slowly work your way around the rug. Depending on the size of your piece, you may have to move the press cloth as you progress around the rug. I start at the edges of my rug but you can start anywhere you please. Give a little extra steam and pressure to areas

that stick up or ripple, especially circles. When your press cloth is almost dry, go back to the sink, rewet it, and continue with pressing and steaming.

When your rug appears to be lying fairly flat, remove the press cloth and flip your rug over to the right side. Rewet your press cloth, but wring it out so there is just a little less moisture than before. Lay the press cloth directly on the right side of your rug and press with a lighter hand. It will take less time to steam the front because you do not need to press as vigorously as you did for the back.

When you have finished steaming, move your rug to a safe place where it can remain undisturbed, and allow it to dry flat, right side up, for 24 hours.

PRELIMINARY STAY STITCHING

After drying completely, your rug's edges are ready to be bound. Regardless of which binding method you choose, you should always do the preliminary stay stitching first. This stitching prevents the foundation cloth from unraveling all the way back to your hooked loops. You can perform the preliminary stay stitching before or after your rug is steam pressed.

A WORD OF CAUTION

Never ever use liquid latex, silicone, or anything else to seal the back of your rug. The chemicals in the latex will damage the foundation and wool loops over time. The rug will be impossible to repair if it suffers any damage. Using a sealant also diminishes the value of your rug significantly.

Straight stitch around the rug.

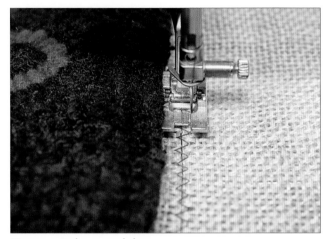
Zigzag stitch around the rug.

Take your hooked piece to a sewing machine. Place the presser foot right up against the outermost row of hooked loops. Straight stitch around the entire perimeter of the rug, taking care that the toe of the presser foot does not get caught in the hooked loops. When you reach the point where you started, switch to a zigzag stitch and sew directly over the line of straight stitching. Move the presser foot over $1/4$" from the previous stitching and sew another row of straight stitches around the entire perimeter, followed by a row of zigzag stitches directly on top of that.

The preliminary stay stitching can also be done around your pattern before you start to hook your rug; however, I prefer to do it afterward. When you are hooking, you sometimes get the inspiration to add, subtract, or alter the original lines of the outer border of the rug. If the stay stitching has been sewn on the foundation cloth first, it would then have to be ripped out and resewn into the proper position to accommodate the new border line. You will save yourself a lot of aggravation if you sew the preliminary stay stitching after your rug is completed.

Stitch and zigzag again.

There are many beautiful binding techniques to finish your raw edges. I have included several of my favorite techniques, and they are listed with the special hooking projects later in this book.

SUPPLIES
A few essential finishing supplies are worth keeping on hand. Gold bent tip tapestry needles are used for whipping yarn around the edges of your rug. The tip is blunt but works like magic to penetrate several layers of foundation cloth and twill tape. I also use this tapestry needle to weave loose ends into my finished edge when crocheting with wool strips (see Chapter 13).

A strong thread is necessary for sewing the binding to the back of your rug. Use a quilting or glazed hand sewing thread for maximum durability.

Binding materials

> ### As a chain is no stronger than its weakest link,
> ### so a hooked rug is no sturdier than its edge.
> Stella Hay Rex, *Practical Hooked Rugs.*

I use regular wool knitting yarn, either worsted weight or bulky, to whip around the edges of my rugs. Choose a yarn that is close to the color of your outside row of hooking. If you cannot get a good match, pick a color that is a shade darker. You can also use 3-ply needlepoint yarn for whipping.

Twill tape binding is used quite often in rug finishing. It is 100% cotton and comes in a $1^1/4$" to $1^1/2$" width. Do not buy iron-on binding. Choose a color that is close to the color of your background. Most of the time, the twill tape binding will not be seen so it does not need to match exactly.

DISPLAYING HOOKED RUGS

Displaying hooked rugs on the wall is a great alternative for projects you don't want to walk on. You must make sure that they are evenly and securely supported so that they do not sag and stretch under their own weight while they are hanging.

A simple technique that I use for hanging hooked rugs is carpet tack strip. Carpet tack strip is a long, 1"-wide, wooden strip with small, sharp nails protruding on an angle through the wood. It can be purchased at any major home improvement or hardware store.

Cut a piece of plywood or fiberboard to the exact measurement of your finished rug. Measure and cut the carpet tack strip so that it fits flush around all four edges on the front surface of the plywood. Make sure you position the wooden strips so the nails are pointed outward, and attach them to the plywood with nails or screws.

To keep the rug flush with the outside edges, I use foam board as filler in the middle. Measure and cut a piece of $1/4$"-thick foam board to fit inside the dimensions of the carpet tack strip. Affix the foam board to the plywood backing with either double-sided tape or glue. Fasten picture-framing wire and hardware to the back of the plywood.

Center your rug and press the finished edges onto the carpet tack strips. You can gently pull on the edges of the rug to secure it to the angled nails. The carpet tack strips will not harm your rug and will hold it securely in place. Hang the entire piece on the wall, just as you would hang a framed picture.

LABELING YOUR RUG

When your binding is completed, take the time to create a label to sew on the back of your rug. You can make a simple label by cutting a piece of muslin or weaver's cloth into a small rectangle. Turn under and press the raw edges.

Use a waterproof acid-free black marker to write on your fabric label. I use the Sakura Pigma Micron pen because it dries fast and doesn't blur or bleed into the fabric. Find these pens online or buy them in craft or artist supply stores.

Include on the label the name of the pattern, your name, the designer of the pattern, and the date you finished hooking the rug.

Rug labels

Write out any additional information that you wish future generations to know about your rug. The label can serve as your identifying hallmark should you ever display your rug at a rug camp or rug exhibit.

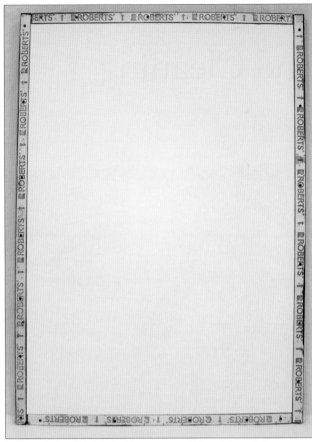

Foam board with tack strips

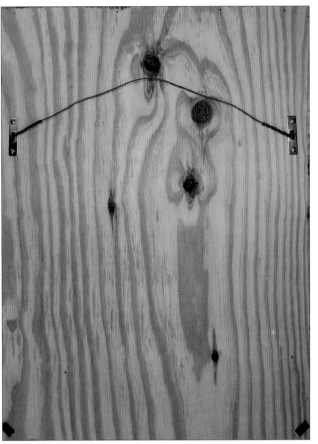

Framing wire and hardware on plywood back

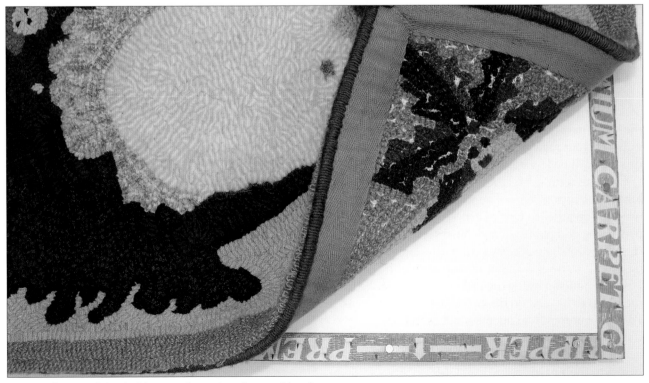

Mounted rug will be held securely to the plywood backing.

CHAPTER 7

Care, Storage, and Cleaning

Roll hooked rugs with the hooked side out.

If you will not be keeping your hooked rug flat on the floor or hanging on the wall, you will need to store it. A hooked rug should never be folded. Folding puts stress on the backing, and over time, these fold lines will become weak, the fibers may break, and the rug could fall apart. Always roll your rug with the hooked side out. Rolling it this way will be less stressful on the foundation cloth.

For long-term storage, wrap your rug in an old pillowcase or cotton sheet. The wool fibers and backing need to "breathe" so never keep a hooked piece in a plastic bag or a plastic storage bin. Store your unused rugs in a cool dry place, away from the dampness of a basement or the extreme heat of an attic.

Use a non-slip waffle rug pad under your hooked rug if it is to be used on hardwood, tile, or slick floors. Protect your rugs from puppies or dogs that chew. Cats are another potential enemy for a hooked rug because their claws can pull out loops with just a few swipes of their paw!

Hooked rugs can be cleaned periodically. You should remove pet hair and dust using a low suction hand vacuum by gently going over the entire rug. Avoid using any type of floor vacuum with super suction or a beater bar that may accidentally catch and pull out your hooked loops. Never vigorously shake or beat a hooked rug.

Gently vacuum the surface.

Dab stains with a damp cloth and mild soap.

Clean soiled areas with mild soap and water. Test a small inconspicuous area first to make sure the colors do not run or bleed when wet. Work up some suds in a small bucket of water and gentle soap. Dab or gently rub the spot with an old clean towel dipped in the soapy solution. Do not saturate the rug. Once you have finished, allow your rug to lie flat for 24 hours to dry completely. Never use cleaners that contain harsh chemicals or bleach.

Never take your rug to a dry cleaner for cleaning. Most of them do not have enough experience or knowledge to properly handle a hooked rug.

Years ago, northern rug hookers cleaned their rugs with snow and many rug hookers today still swear by this method. Wait for a winter day when there is a fresh snowfall. The snow must be dry and powdery. If it won't pack and you can't form a snowball with it, this is the perfect consistency. Lay your rug face down in the snow. Gently brush some of the powdery snow over it with a broom. Move a thin layer of snow over the rug and then brush it away. Turn the rug over so it is face up (hooked side up) and gently brush snow over it again. Make sure you carefully go over the entire rug, then brush off the excess. When you lift your rug up, a ring of dirt will remain in the snow. Bring the rug into the house and let it dry flat for 24 hours.

Snow cleaning a rug: to surface clean, brush on snow, then brush it off.

PART TWO

The Projects

CHAPTER 8

A Lesson on Basic Rug Hooking:
Hearts and Flowers

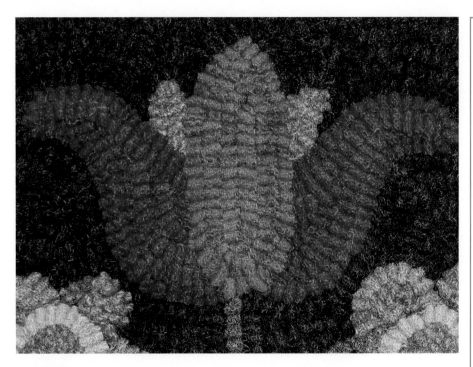

MATERIALS
(finished size: 9" x 12")

- Foundation cloth of your choice, cut to 20" x 20"

- 4" x 15¹/₂" piece of light red wool for the middle petal of the tulip and flourishes on sides of heart

- 8" x 15" piece of dark red wool for the outer tulip petals and the outside of the heart

- 5" x 16" piece of red-orange wool for the small tulip petals and the small flower centers

- 5" x 17" piece of coral/orange/green plaid for the small flower petals and the inner accent line on heart

- 2" x 16¹/₂" piece of gold wool for the outline around the small flower centers

- 1¹/₂" x 16¹/₂" piece of green wool for the tulip and flower stems

- 31" x 16¹/₂" piece of black/dark green check wool for the background

- 1³/₈ yards 1¹/₄" wide black cotton twill tape for binding edges

- 18 yards of black wool bulky weight yarn for whipping edges

T his little mat is the perfect size for a first project. It will hook up quickly and you will learn the basic techniques for hooking curves, angles, circles, straight lines, and square corners. Cut your wool in a #8 size except where noted. The wool amounts listed are general estimates. Your results may vary depending on how high or low you hook.

The finished size of the rug is 9" x 12". Cutting your foundation cloth to a measurement of 20" x 20" will allow at least 4" of excess material around each side of the pattern. Transfer the design to the backing of your choice with a waterproof marker. Refer to Chapter 5 for details on drawing patterns. Stretch your pattern tightly over a rug hooking frame or hoop.

GETTING STARTED

One of the most often asked questions is, "Where do I begin?" It is best to start hooking with the shapes in the foreground or with an object that is on the top. In *Hearts and Flowers*, the middle tulip petal is on top of all the other tulip petals.

Choose a spot on the left side of the petal. Avoid starting at the tip of the flower where a cut end would look awkward. Hold a light red wool strip in your left hand underneath the foundation cloth and directly below where you want to pull up your first loop.

Hearts and Flowers, 9" x 12", #8-cut wool on linen.
Designed and hooked by Kris Miller, Howell, Michigan, 2014.

Hearts and Flowers, © 2013 Kris Miller, enlarge to 9" x 12".

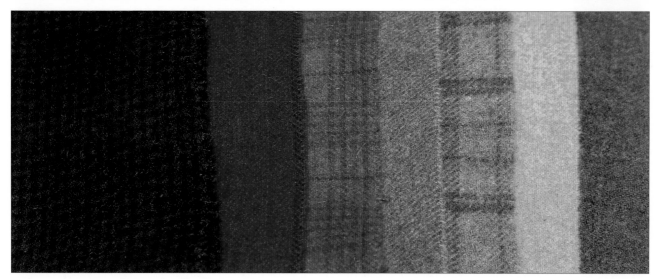

Color swatches used to make *Hearts and Flowers*.

1. Stay just inside the drawn line. Push your hook down through the foundation, scooping up the end of the strip.

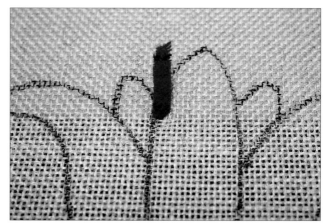

2. Pull the end to the top of your work, leaving about a ½" tail.

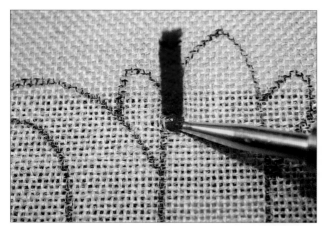

3. Now push your hook down into the very next hole in the foundation and grab the strip.

4. Pull a loop of wool up to the top of your work to a height of ¼".

5. Skip one hole in the foundation. Push your hook down into the second hole, scoop up the wool, and pull up another loop ¼" high.

6. Continue hooking loops, skipping every other hole.

7. When you get to the curve at the bottom of the petal, push your hook down into the hole that is diagonally to the right from the straight row you are hooking and pull up a loop.

8. Try to skip every other hole or measure over by counting two threads in the foundation cloth. If the loops look too far apart, you can hook in every diagonal hole until you get around the curve. It will help if you turn your frame or hoop as you are working.

9. When you come to the end of your wool strip, pull the tail up to the top. It should come up in the next hole right after the last loop you hooked.

10. Start another strip by pulling up the new end in the same hole where the last strip ended. You will have two ends occupying one hole.

11. Pull up a loop in the very next hole and continue hooking, skipping every other hole for the remainder of the strip.

12. When you get to the top of the petal, hook a loop at the tip.

13. Turn your frame or hoop. Count down two diagonal threads, push your hook down into the foundation, and pull up a loop.

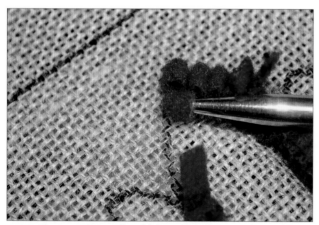

14. The new loop should be almost at a right angle to the previous one. Make sure you pull the loop up tight so there isn't a lump underneath it.

15. Continue to hook down the edge of the petal.

16. When you get back to where you started, pull up the end of the current strip in the same hole where you pulled up the first end.

17. Snip off the ends so they are even with the hooked loops.

18. Begin filling in the petal. Starting at the narrow tip of the petal, pull up the end of a new strip and begin hooking loops beside the outer row.

19. The shoulders of your loops should touch but not "hug" the previous row.

> ### TIP
>
> *If the rows are too close, the loops will crush each other. If the rows are too far apart, you will see the foundation. Usually if you count over two or three threads in the foundation, you will get the correct spacing.*

20. Hook all the way around the petal until you get back to the tip. Pull up the end of your strip and cut it off. Begin another row by pulling up the end of a new strip in the angle formed where the previous two rows of loops come together.

21. Continue hooking rows until the center petal is completely filled.

22. Use the dark red wool to outline the outer tulip petal on the left. Start by pulling up an end right next to the base of the center petal and hook along the outer edge of the petal, staying just inside the drawn line.

23. When you get to the tip, hook around the narrow curve.

24. You may have to pull up a loop in nearly every hole until you have completed the tip.

25. Once the outline is worked in, pull up the end of your strip so that it abuts the side of the center petal. Fill in the next inside row of the outer petal.

26. When you hook up to the tip of the petal, bring the end up and cut it.

27. Then start hooking a new strip just below it.

28. Follow along the curves until the petal is entirely filled in. Repeat the same process for the outer petal on the opposite side.

29. The small tulip petals are hooked with the red orange wool. Start at the narrow angle between the red petals and hook around the curve at the top, ending against the side of a larger petal. The red orange petals are small enough that the outline will cover the area without the need for filling in any additional space.

1. The smaller heart is on top of the larger one and should be hooked first. Use the coral/orange/green plaid wool to outline the smaller heart. Start hooking your strip on one side and directly on the line.

2. When you come to the point at the bottom, hook one loop, turn your frame, bring your hook over two threads diagonally, and pull up a loop that is perpendicular to the previous loop.

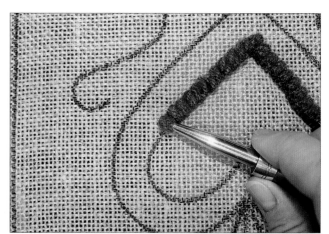

3. Continue outlining the small heart around the curve until you get to the angle at the top of the heart.

4. Hook one loop just past the point of the angle, turn your frame, skip two threads in your foundation, and pull up a loop at a right angle to the previous loop.

5. Continue around the curve of the heart until you have reached your starting point.

6. Pull the end of your current strip up into the same hole where you placed the end of your first strip. There will be two ends in one hole. Trim them evenly with the other hooked loops.

7. Fill the smaller heart with the red-orange wool, hooking the first row beside the plaid outline.

8. Take care to stagger your cut ends so they do not line up together from row to row. Hook down to the bottom point of the heart.

9. Turn your frame, move your hook over a thread or two, and pull up a new loop perpendicular to the previous loop.

10. Continue hooking up the side of the heart.

11. When you get to the top, gently curve your loops around the angle.

12. Keep working with the red-orange wool until the empty spaces are completely filled in.

13. Use the dark red wool to outline the larger heart by hooking just inside the drawn line.

14. Work the bottom point and the top angle in exactly the same way as you did for the plaid outline of the smaller heart.

15. Now work one row of the dark red wool up against the plaid outline of the smaller heart.

16. Once this row is hooked, you will notice a few small, open, unhooked areas that need to be filled in with additional dark red wool.

17. You can hand cut your wool to a narrower width for filling in these areas.

Hook the Flowers

1. Flowers are easier to hook if you work from the center out to the petals. Use the red-orange wool to outline the center circle.

2. Once the outline is completed, hook the empty spot in the center by pulling up an end, hooking two loops, and pulling up the other end.

TIP

When hooking a circle, you may have to hook in every hole occasionally so that the loops are not spaced too far apart. When you get back to the point where you started, pull up the end of your current strip in the same hole where you started so there are two ends in one hole. To fill the circle, follow the curve of the circle and keep the loops fairly snug against the previous row. Remember, you may have to hook a loop in every hole occasionally.

3. Hook one row of gold wool around the flower center. Follow the curve of the center circle, and end with two ends in the starting hole. Snip off the tails so the ends are flush with the hooked loops.

4. Using the coral/orange/green plaid wool, outline a flower petal.

5. Hook all the petals so that your cut ends begin and end along the outer gold circle. Once your outline is completed, fill in the petals with the plaid.

6. Hook the second small flower using the same method as you did for the first.

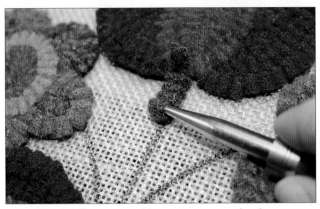

1. After the flowers and hearts are completely hooked, use the green wool to hook the flower stems. Hook the center stem first by starting at the base of the tulip and working a single line of loops down to the middle of the heart. Hook directly on the drawn line.

2. Start the two side stems at the base of the small flowers and hook directly on the drawn line down to the middle of the heart. Trim all your ends so they are even with your work.

3. Hook one row of background around all of the motifs, using the black/dark green check.

4. When you work down into a sharp angle or tight spot, end your strip by pulling a tail up to the top of your work.

5. Begin a new strip by pulling up its end close to the neighboring row of hooked loops and then continue to work around the shapes.

TIP

I hook two straight rows around the outer perimeter of my rugs because it provides a stable edge for binding later. However, when the design is close to the edge and it is not possible to make two rows, one row of hooked loops will suffice to stabilize your work.

6. As you are hooking around the small flowers, you will get close to the outer edge of the mat.

7. Stop filling and hook one straight row of background at the edge, staying just inside the drawn line.

8. Once you have hooked a short length down the outside edge, you can return to filling in the background again.

9. When you have completed hooking one row of background around everything, work in the flourishes next to the heart. Use the light red wool and hook directly on the drawn line.

10. Immediately work one row of black background around the flourishes to preserve their shape, hooking in a gentle curve around the ends.

11. I delayed snipping off the tails of the flourishes until the area around them was completely filled in. Hook and fill any small empty spots in the immediate area.

12. Begin filling in the remaining empty spaces of the background. Hook around all the shapes, following their contours. Simultaneously work in two straight rows around the outer perimeter whenever possible.

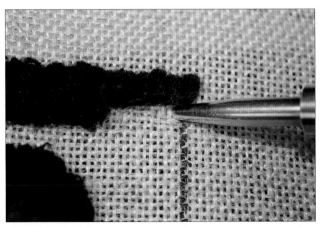

13. Hook right up to the perpendicular lines that form the corner.

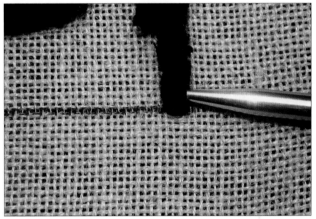

14. Now hook one more loop in the hole that is just beyond the drawn line.

15. Turn your frame. Find a hole that is just inside the drawn line, on the diagonal from the corner loop, and approximately two threads from your previous hooked row.

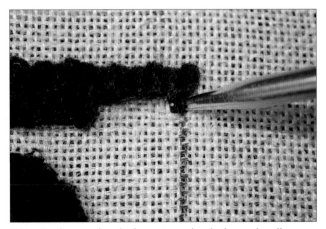

16. Push your hook down into this hole and pull up a loop.

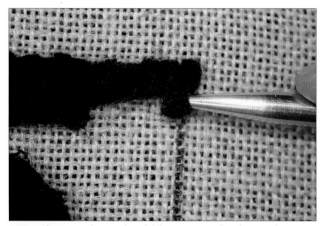

17. The new loop should be perpendicular to the loop in the corner.

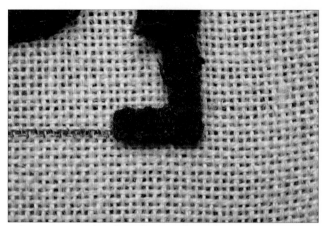

18. Continue hooking loops along the new row.

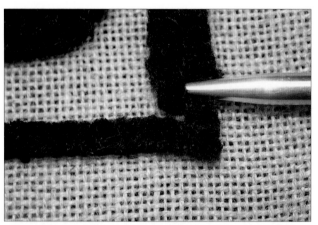

19. When hooking the second row along the edge, create a turned corner in the same manner. Hook all the way up to the corner.

20. Turn your frame. Locate a hole that is about two threads away from the previous row and on a diagonal from the last loop you hooked.

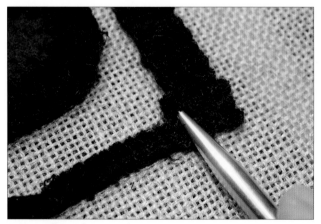

21. Pull up the new loop.

22. It should be perpendicular to the previous loop and there should be two to three threads in between the new loop and the outermost row. Continue hooking the second row around the edge.

When all your hooking is done, trim any loose threads that have come up to the top of your work. Turn your mat over and examine the back of it. You should see some areas where the foundation is showing in between the rows of hooking. This is normal and means you have not packed your loops or rows too tightly. A hooked rug needs these small spaces to "breathe." However, sometimes you will find a larger empty spot where you have forgotten to hook. These spots are called "holidays."

1 There is a triangular holiday to the right of the heart.

2 Mark the spot by sticking a toothpick into the holiday. Push the toothpick from the back to the front.

3 Flip your mat back over to the right side. The toothpick will reveal the area where you need to fill with a few more loops.

4 Remove the toothpick and fill with a few loops of the appropriate color.

Steam press your mat, both back and front, and allow it to dry. Sew two rows of preliminary stay stitching around the entire mat (*refer to Chapter 6*).

One of my favorite binding techniques is to whip the edge with yarn and attach the twill tape binding simultaneously. It creates a beautiful finish and saves time by eliminating a step in the sewing process.

You will need 1¼" wide cotton twill tape binding in a coordinating color. It does not need to match perfectly because it will not be visible from the front. Measure around your mat's edge and add approximately 6" to this measurement. Washing twill tape prior to use is optional, but if you do wash the tape,

allow another 4" per yard for shrinkage.

Choose a coordinating wool yarn for whipping. You will want a color that matches closely with the outer row of your hooked edge. When in doubt, choose a color that is just slightly darker. I prefer to use a bulky weight yarn, but worsted weight yarn will work just as well. To estimate how much yarn you need, measure around the perimeter of your mat. For every inch of mat, you will need 12 inches of yarn. If you use a double strand of yarn, double your measurements. I always add a little extra to my yarn measurement so I do not run short and have trouble matching the color later.

1. Do not start in a corner. I start in an inconspicuous spot, such as the left lower edge. Fold the edge of your foundation cloth toward the back of your mat, leaving a scant ¼" lip.

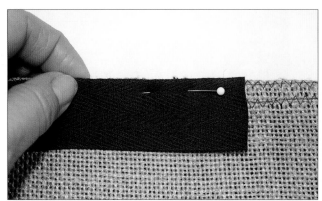

2. Working from the wrong side, pin the twill tape along the folded edge.

3. Thread a length of yarn through a tapestry needle. Do not knot the end. Starting 1½" from the cut edge of the twill tape, insert the tapestry needle approximately ¼" from the top.

4. Push it through both the twill tape and the foundation, coming up on the other side at the feet of the loops (not in between the loops).

5. Pull the yarn through, leaving about a 2" tail. Hold this tail along the top of the fold, bring the needle around to the back, and insert it into the twill tape again, placing it as close as possible to the last stitch.

6. Pull the yarn through and continue whipping, encasing the folded edge and the tail of yarn. Make sure your stitches are close enough so that they completely cover the foundation cloth. When your yarn becomes too short, slip the tapestry needle back through the previously whipped stitches and cut off the end of the yarn.

7. Begin with a new length of yarn and continue whipping the edge of the mat, encasing the tail of the yarn at the same time.

8. When you are within 4" of the corner, stop whipping and open up the foundation cloth. Carefully trim away the excess foundation as shown here.

9. Fold the trimmed corner, making it square and maintaining the ¼" folded lip. Place a pin in the corner.

10. To miter the corner, hold the twill tape along the folded edge so it extends out beyond the corner.

11. Make a fold exactly in line with the side edge of the mat. Place your thumb on the fold and then pull the leading edge of the twill tape down so that it is lying along the side edge.

12. You will create a right angle and a neatly pointed tip. Pin through the twill tape and foundation to hold the tape in place.

13. Whip the yarn up to the corner.

14. When you get to the very tip, stitch in the same hole several times and fan out the yarn so it completely covers the point. You may have to manipulate the yarn with your fingers to cover all of the foundation.

15. Remove the pin from the corner after you secure the corner with the whipped stitches. Continue whipping the edges and corners. When you are approximately 4" from the point where you started, prepare the ends of the twill tape so they will join neatly. Open up the leading edge of the twill tape so that it overlaps the starting point by about 2" and cut off any excess tape.

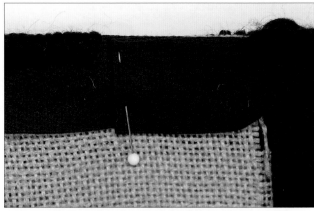

16. Fold the leading edge of the twill tape under about 1", and pin it on top of the starting edge.

17. Continue whipping until the yarn has completely covered the edge.

18. Slip the tapestry needle through several whipped stitches and cut off the excess yarn.

19. Fold back the loose edge of the twill tape and CAREFULLY cut off the excess foundation. Trim it to about 1″ width so that the foundation will be hidden under the twill tape.

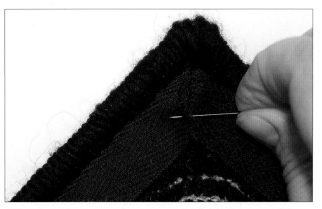

20. Sew the mitered corners and folded seam of the twill tape with sewing needle and thread, using a whipstitch.

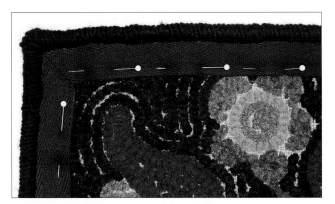

21. Pin the loose edges of the twill tape to the mat.

22. Use a needle and thread to whipstitch the edges, taking care to insert the needle deep enough to pick up a thread of the foundation. Do not sew only through a wool loop.

23. When your binding is completed, lightly steam press the edges of your mat (*refer to Chapter 6*), both front and back.

CHAPTER 9

A Lesson on Hooking Points:
Lucky Stars Chair Pad

MATERIALS
(finished size: 14" in diameter)

- Foundation cloth of your choice, cut to 22" x 22"

- 3" x 16" piece of gold wool for stars

- 5$\frac{1}{2}$" x 16" piece of grass green wool for stars

- 6" x 16$\frac{1}{2}$" piece of turquoise wool for stars

- 1$\frac{1}{2}$" x 17" piece of turquoise/gold plaid for stars

- 2" x 16" piece of red/beige textured wool for stars

- 6$\frac{1}{2}$" x 15" piece of barn red plaid wool for stars

- 1" x 16" piece of celery green textured wool for stars

- 4" x 15$\frac{1}{2}$" piece of cream/taupe plaid wool for center circle of background

- 12" x 16$\frac{1}{2}$" piece of oatmeal wool for middle circle of background

- $\frac{3}{8}$ yard of dark taupe plaid wool for outer circle of background

- 20 yards taupe bulky weight wool yarn for whipping the edges

Stars are one of the most popular design motifs among rug hookers. Stars with nice, crisp points might seem difficult, but if you follow some basic tips, your hooked stars will shine with perfection! This technique will also work for similarly angled objects such as triangles, bird beaks and wings, pointed animal ears, pointed leaf tips, and flower petals.

This fun little chair pad is a candidate for many different color plans. Alternative choices are bright tropical hues, primitive neutral shades, or patriotic red, white, and blue. The key to unifying the design is to choose a color that is used in one star and repeat it again in the other two. In my chair pad, gold appears in a different area of each star. This color serves as a common denominator and encourages the viewer's eyes to move around the design.

Cut your wool in #8 size strips. The wool amounts listed are general estimates. Your needs may vary depending on how high or low you hook.

The finished diameter of the chair pad is 14". Cutting your foundation cloth to a measurement of 22" x 22" will allow 4" of excess material around each side of the pattern. Make sure that the grain of the foundation cloth is straight both horizontally and vertically as you line up your pattern. Transfer the design to the foundation cloth with a waterproof marker. Refer to Chapter 5 on drawing patterns for details. Stretch your pattern tightly over a rug hooking frame or hoop.

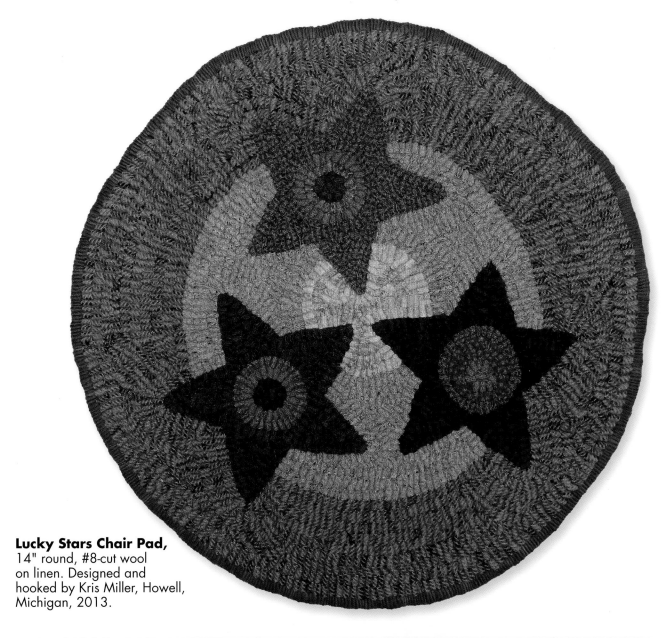

Lucky Stars Chair Pad,
14" round, #8-cut wool
on linen. Designed and
hooked by Kris Miller, Howell,
Michigan, 2013.

Hook the Stars

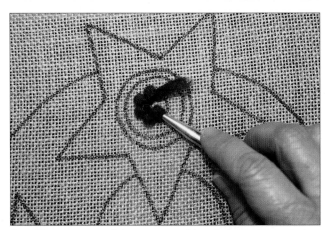

1. Choose one of the stars and hook the center circle with the grass green wool. Outline by hooking just inside the drawn line.

2. Fill in the small empty portion in the center by pulling up an end, hooking one loop, and then pulling up the other end.

Lucky Stars Chair Pad,
© 2013 Kris Miller,
enlarge to 14" round.

3. Using the turquoise/gold plaid, hook one row around the green center and then hook a row of gold wool around that.

Creating Sharp Points

You should never have cut ends at the tips of your star points. Not only would your eye always be drawn to those spots, the tips would not have a crisp angle. Let me show you a great trick for getting sharp points to a star.

1 Hold a turquoise wool strip in your left hand, grasping it in the middle so that both ends are hanging down equally.

2 Position your left hand under the foundation cloth, directly under the tip of the star. Push your hook through the foundation cloth, and pull up one loop from the strip underneath to the height of about ¹/₄".

3 Allow your left hand to grab one of the ends hanging down underneath your work and use it to hook a row of loops down one side of the star point, taking care to stay just inside the drawn line. When you get to the end of the strip, pull the tail up to the top.

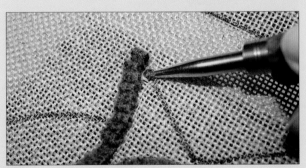

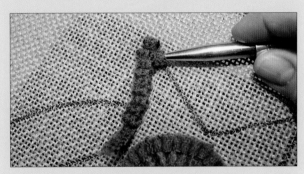

4 Now direct your attention to the other half of the strip. The first loop you have pulled up will be the tip of the star. Hook a second loop from the remaining length, just down from the tip and directly adjacent to the other loop so only one foundation thread lies between the two. You will have to drop down a hole or two in your foundation cloth to find the correct placement.

5 Continue hooking down the other side of the star point until you come to the end of your strip and then pull the tail to the top.

6 Work the other four star points the same way.

4. Once all the star points are completed, go back and finish outlining the star, connecting all of the tails.

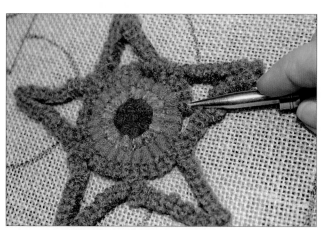

5. Hook one row of turquoise wool around the circles in the middle of the star. If you come to a spot where the star outline touches the center circles, end your strip and begin hooking on the other side.

6. Fill in the star points. Using the turquoise wool and starting at the tip, hook a row along each side of the star point.

7. Continue hooking rows from the tip to the center until the star point is completely filled in.

8. Repeat for the other four star points.

9. For the second star, hook the center circle with the gold wool.

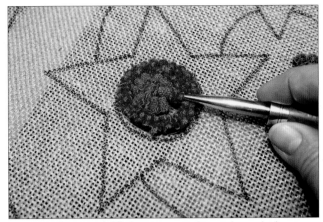

10. Outline and fill the next inside circle with the red/beige texture.

11. Hook one row of turquoise wool around the two circles you just created.

12. Starting at a star tip, use the barn red wool to outline and fill the star, using the same technique as the turquoise star.

13. Use the barn red wool to outline and fill the center circle of the third star.

14. Work one row of gold wool around the center circle, then one row of celery green wool around the gold.

15. Use the grass green wool to hook the star tips first, then outline and fill the rest of the star, using the same technique as you did for the previous two stars.

16. Once all three stars are completed, hook the background. Start with the center circle and work your way out to the edge of the chair pad. Using the cream/taupe plaid, outline the center circle, staying just inside the drawn line.

17. When you come to the point of a star, make a turn with your wool strip and hook along the edge until you come to the star tip.

18. Hook your loops close to the tip.

19. This is one time when you can "break the rules" and hook in every hole if necessary. Crowding your stitches just a little bit in this area will help maintain the shape of the tip.

20. Continue outlining around the center circle, hooking around the star points and tips until you come back to the place you started. When the center circle is outlined, hook all the small, empty spaces until the area is completely filled in.

21. Using the oatmeal wool, hook the middle circle of the chair pad.

22. Start by outlining all the way around the perimeter, staying just inside the drawn line. Notice that the three stars intersect the middle circle so you will have three separate sections to complete. Outline the star and then hook the star points and tips, hooking around and around the shapes until they are filled in.

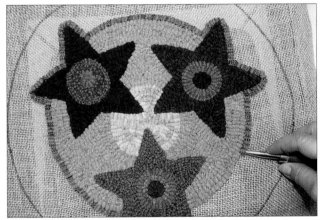

23. Hook the outer circle last. Use the dark taupe plaid and hook one row against the middle circle and stars. Work in continuous rows by following around the shapes of the stars and middle circle. If there are no shapes to hook around, just follow the contour of the circle, making long, straight rows.

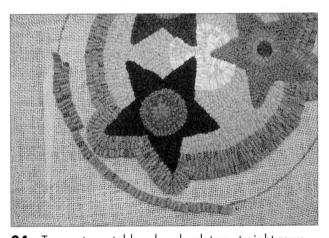

24. To create a stable edge, hook two straight rows around the outermost perimeter of the chair pad. You will come to a point where you will have to work in these two rows simultaneously as you are hooking and filling in the outer circle. Hook the two border rows for a short length and then fill in some of your background up to the border.

25. By working simultaneously on both the border and background, your foundation cloth will have some room to stretch and it will lessen the chance of having your chair pad ripple. When the hooking is completed, turn your chair pad over and check for any holidays (*refer to Chapter 8*).

Steam press your chair pad back and front and allow it to dry. Sew two rows of preliminary stay stitching around the outer perimeter (*refer to Chapter 6 on finishing*).

Whipping the edges with yarn is a simple and easy finish. Folding the foundation and then whipping around it creates a rounded edge that imitates the use of cording.

Choose a coordinating wool yarn for whipping. Use a color that matches closely with the outer row of your hooked edge. I often choose a color that is just slightly darker. Bulky weight yarn is a good choice. You can use worsted weight but you may find that you need to double the yarn. To estimate how much yarn you need, measure around the perimeter of your chair pad. For every inch measured, you will need 12 inches of yarn. (You must double your measurements if you use a double strand.) Always add a little extra yardage to the yarn measurement so you do not run short.

1. To prepare the edges for whipping, first measure 1¹/₂" from the outermost hooked row and mark it with a waterproof marker or pencil. Mark around the entire perimeter of the chair pad.

2. Cut off the excess foundation cloth using a sharp pair of scissors and following the marked lines.

3. Working from the right side, fold the cut foundation cloth in half.

4. Fold it in half again, ease in any excess material as you fold around the curves, and secure with straight pins.

5. Baste the pinned edges in place with a running stitch, using a sewing needle and thread.

6. Thread a length of yarn through a large-eyed tapestry needle. Working from the right side of the chair pad, push the tapestry needle down through a hole in the foundation that is very close to a hooked loop, but not in the same hole as the hooked loop.

7. Pull the yarn all the way through the foundation, leaving about a 2" tail. Hold this tail along the folded edge.

8. Bring the needle and yarn around the folded edge to the front of the chair pad. Push the needle down into the foundation cloth right next to the first whipped stitch.

9. Continue to whip the yarn around the folded edge, encasing the tail and completely covering the exposed edge of the foundation.

10. When you have used up the length of yarn, thread the tapestry needle back through some of the previous whipped stitches and cut off the excess yarn.

11. Begin a new length of yarn, leaving another 2" tail along the edge.

12. Continue whipping, encasing the tail inside the stitches. When you have whipped all the way around, slip your tapestry needle through several of the previous whipped stitches and cut off the excess yarn.

13. Once your chair pad is completely bound, it may be a little rippled because you whipped around areas that were on the bias of the foundation cloth. This is normal. Giving your piece another thorough steaming (*refer to Chapter 6*) following the binding process should smooth out and flatten the edges.

CHAPTER 10

A Lesson on Creating Dimension with Directional Hooking: Moonlight Glow

MATERIALS
(finished size: 21¹/₂" x 14¹/₂")

- Foundation cloth of your choice, cut to 30" x 23"

- 1" x 17" piece of brown plaid (#6 cut) for cat's nose

- 4" x 16¹/₂" piece of charcoal herringbone (#6 cut) for cat's mouth and leg outline

- One strip, 16" long, of dark red wool (#6 cut) for the cat's mouth

- 3" x 17" piece of medium gray (#8 cut) for the cat's muzzle and inner ear

- 14" x 17" piece of antique black (#8 cut) for cat's head and body

- 1 strip of antique black 17" long (#6 cut) for cat's eyes

- 2 strips of cream colored wool 16" long (#8 cut) for cat's eyes

- 14" x 16" piece of pale gold wool (#8 cut) for moon

- 6" x 16" piece of rust plaid (#8 cut) for the pumpkin outline

- 4 different shades and/or textures of orange, each measuring 7" x 15" (#8 and #8.5 cuts) for filling in the pumpkin

- 4¹/₂" x 16" piece of gold wool (#8 cut) for pumpkin eyes, nose, and mouth

- ¹/₂ yard piece of purple wool plaid (#8.5 cut) for background

The direction in which your wool strips are hooked has great impact and influence on the mood and overall appearance of your rug. Hooking in straight rows evokes feelings of calmness, stillness, and quiet and makes things look flat. Curving rows suggests dimension and shape or creates movement and excitement. Since rug hooking is a two-dimensional art, we rely on the direction of our hooking to keep our eyes moving around the design. It gives life and character to our rugs.

You can mix different-sized cut strips in one rug. Smaller cuts are needed for fine details that would otherwise look too chunky and overpowering with a larger size strip. Take advantage of the beautiful colors and woven patterns in plaids, stripes, and other textures. They retain their characteristics better in a wider cut. In *Moonlight Glow*, cutting the orange wool strips in a #8.5 cut adds to the texture and shape of the pumpkin. The beautiful purple plaid background also benefits from a larger strip size.

While the rule is to hook your strips as high as they are wide, it changes just a little bit when you combine a variety of width sizes. All the loops should be as high as the widest strip used in a single project. Simply said, just make sure all your loops are pulled up to the same height, regardless of their width.

Cut the wool in the sizes listed. The wool amounts listed are general estimates. Your needs may vary depending on how high or low you hook.

The finished size of the rug is 21¹/₂" x 14¹/₂". Cutting your foundation cloth to a measurement of 30" x 23" will allow 4" of excess material around each side of the pattern. Transfer the design to the backing of your choice with a waterproof marker. Refer to Chapter 5 on drawing patterns for details. Stretch your pattern tightly over a rug hooking frame or hoop.

Moonlight Glow, 21½" x 14½", #6-, 8-, 8.5-cut wool on linen.
Designed and hooked by Kris Miller, Howell, Michigan, 2014.

Moonlight Glow, © 2013 Kris Miller, enlarge to 21¹/₂" x 14¹/₂".

Sometimes the best place to start a rug is on the face. It is usually the most difficult element of a rug. Not only will you overcome this hurdle right away, but you will love how the completed hooked face will instantly give your project more character. There is nothing more pleasant than to have a happy face smiling back at you as you work!

1. Begin with the strip of brown plaid to hook the cat's nose. Hook a few loops for the nose and then work in the line underneath the nose.

2. Hook the upper part of cat's mouth directly on the drawn line with a strip of charcoal herringbone.

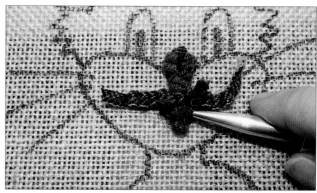

3. Use dark red wool to hook the lower part of the mouth. Do not overhook this area. Three loops hooked in a triangular shape should be sufficient.

4. Using the medium gray wool, outline the muzzle.

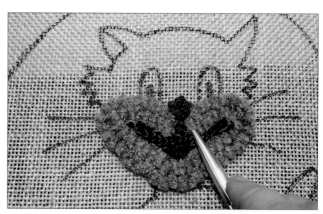

5. Fill in the muzzle, following its curved shape.

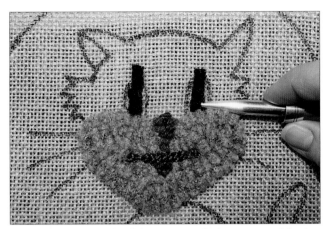

6. Hook the pupils of the eyes with the antique black wool. Notice that they are merely three loops that are worked perpendicular to the top of the muzzle.

7. Immediately hook around the pupils with the cream colored wool.

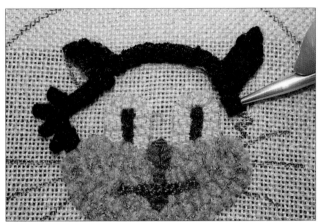

8. Using the antique black wool, outline around the cat's head. Start at one side of the muzzle and hook around to the other side. The areas of hair tufts on the side of the cat's head are worked first by hooking a loop in the outline area.

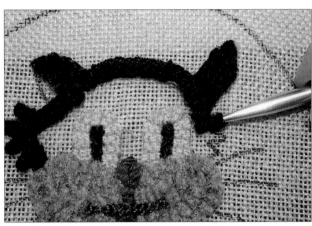

9. Next, skip over to a hole in the foundation that is directly outside the head but closely adjacent to this loop. Push your hook down into the hole and pull up a loop.

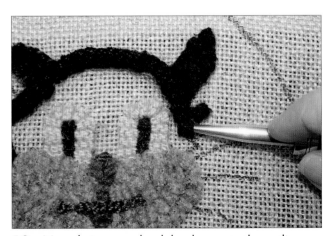

10. Now, bring your hook back over to the outline area and pull up another loop.

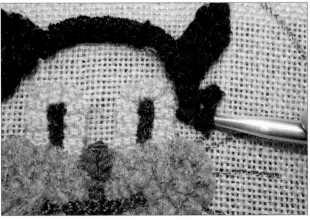

11. Finally, skip over to an adjacent outside hole in the foundation and pull up a loop.

12. Repeat this process again until the hair tufts on each side of the cat's head are completed.

13. Outline around the cat's eyes.

14. Then fill in the open areas of the head, hooking along the curves directionally.

15. The last step for completing the cat's head is to hook the inside of the left ear, using the medium gray wool.

16. Since the cat is black and the legs are drawn so that they are in front of the cat's body, the legs must be outlined with a contrasting wool color so they will remain visible after the cat is completely hooked. Use the charcoal herringbone to outline down the left shoulder, along both legs, and around the paws. Hook directly on the drawn line.

17. Outline the rest of the cat's body with the antique black, working up one side of the tail, gently rounding the tip, and hooking down the other side.

18. While filling in the rest of the cat, consider the body contours and the way the fur would grow. Begin just below the chin and hook straight down into the legs, filling in the toes of the paws.

19. Hook the hip lines with curved rows from top to bottom.

20. Any additional small open areas should be filled in directionally too.

21. Once the cat is completed, hook one row of outline around the moon using the pale gold wool.

22. The whiskers are worked next and should be hooked directly on the drawn line using strips of charcoal herringbone wool.

23. Immediately hook one row of pale gold wool around the outside of the cat's body, head, and whiskers.

24. When you get to the area of the hair tufts, fill around them. Hook a loop next to the tuft, skip over to the hole in between two hair tufts, push your hook down into a hole, and pull up a loop of pale gold wool.

25. Jump back over and hook another pale gold loop next to the outside of the second hair tuft. Repeat the process until the tufted hair areas are completely filled in. You should be moving your hook over to each adjacent hole, and you should have no lumps or long floats on the bottom of your work.

26. To maximize the characteristics of the full moon, hook it following the curve of the circle.

27. There are a few small areas around the cat that cannot be filled in this way but if the majority of the hooking is done directionally, the roundness will still be implied.

28. Outline the pumpkin with the rust plaid. Stay just inside the drawn lines for the outline. However, when hooking the curved accent lines in the body of the pumpkin, hook directly on the line.

29. Mix the four different values of #8.5-cut orange wool in one pile. Draw a strip out of the pile randomly, and begin to fill in the pumpkin. Start at the top of the pumpkin and hook each row directionally down to the bottom.

30. Work both sides of the pumpkin evenly.

31. Take care to stagger the ends of your strips so that they do not line up in the same area as you are hooking. When you come to a hooked rust plaid accent line, use a strip of orange wool cut into a #8 width and connect the lines together. Continue hooking from the top to the bottom of the pumpkin, filling in the space until you reach the facial features.

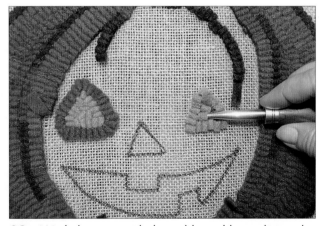

32. Work the eyes with the gold wool by outlining the triangular shapes and filling them in. Immediately hook around the eyes with one row of orange wool.

33. The nose is worked in the same manner as the eyes. The mouth is also hooked with gold wool. Outline around the mouth, staying just inside the drawn line, then fill it in.

34. Hook one row of orange wool around the mouth.

35. Work in the teeth by hooking straight rows across the area.

36. Once the facial features are completed, fill in the pumpkin until your directional hooking reaches the outline of the eyes.

37. Hook a straight line down the middle, from the top of the pumpkin to the middle of the nose. You can draw this line with a permanent marker or just follow along the grain of your foundation cloth. This is a perspective line that will help bridge the curved directional lines on both sides and will give better dimension to the pumpkin.

38. I hooked three of these straight lines and then filled in the rest of the small empty areas with more orange wool strips until the pumpkin was completed.

39. Hook one row of purple plaid background wool around all the shapes.

40. Hook around the moon and cat and then fill in the small open area next to the cat's tail.

41. While working the background around the pumpkin, hook one straight row along the bottom borderline of the rug. Fill in between the pumpkin and this border line.

42. I hooked two rows of background around all the other outside edges as I was filling.

43. Work around all the objects with gently curving lines, echoing around the shapes as you hook until the entire background is filled in.

44. Turn your rug over and check for any holidays. Steam press your rug on both back and front and allow it to dry. Bind the edges. (*Refer to Chapters 6 and 8.*)

CHAPTER 11

A Lesson on Hooking Letters:
Snow Day

MATERIALS
(finished size: 21" x 14")

- Foundation cloth of your choice, cut to 29" x 22"

- 3" x 16" piece of antique black wool (one #4 strip, one #6 strip, remainder #8 cuts) for hat, eyes, mouth, and buttons

- One strip of red wool for hatband, cut in a #8 width

- One strip of orange wool (#6 cut) for the carrot nose

- 2½" x 16" piece of light gray herringbone (#6 cut) for the body outline

- 8" x 15" piece of off-white textured wool (#8 cut) for snowman's body

- 1½" x 16" piece of brown textured wool (#6 cut) for arms

- 10" x 16½" piece of blue and white herringbone (#8 cut) for the letters

- 1 yard of dark teal blue windowpane plaid (#8 cut) for the background

When I was a beginner, the idea of hooking letters paralyzed me: I was afraid that they might sink into my background and become unreadable. But if you stop to consider that letters are just single straight lines, much like an ordinary border line or a flower stem, they suddenly become much more manageable. Follow these simple suggestions and you will be hooking letters like a pro in no time.

The wool amounts listed are general estimates. Your results may vary depending on how high or low you hook.

The finished size of the rug is 21" x 14". Cutting your foundation cloth to a measurement of 29" x 22" will allow 4" of excess material around each side of the pattern. Transfer the design to the backing of your choice with a waterproof marker. Refer to Chapter 5 on drawing patterns. Stretch your pattern tightly over a rug hooking frame or hoop.

Hook the Snowman

1. The snowman's arms cross over the letters N and W, so it is easiest to hook the snowman first and the letters afterward. Using antique black, hook the brim of the snowman's hat.

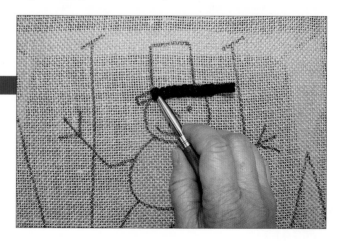

Snow Day, 21" x 14", #4-, 6-, and 8-cut wool on linen, designed and hooked by Kris Miller, Howell, Michigan, 2013.

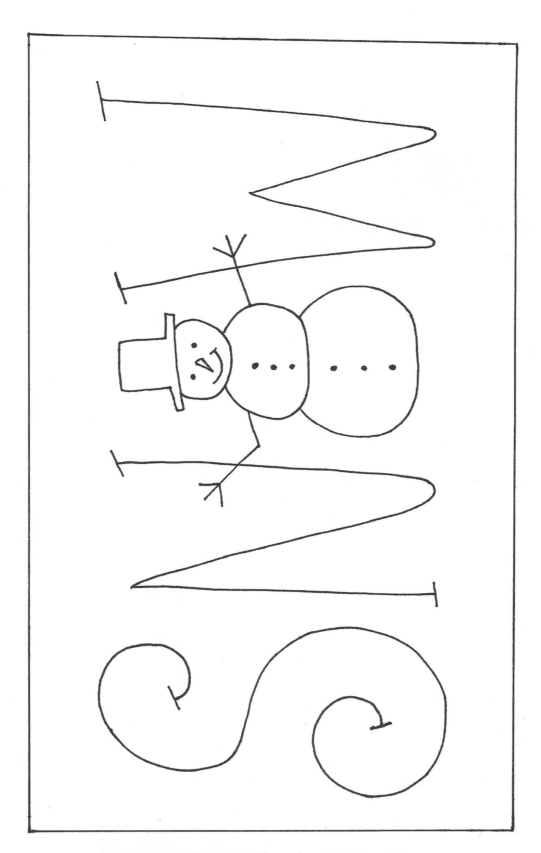

Snow Day, © 2013 Kris Miller, enlarge to 21" x 14".

2. Use a strip of red wool cut in a #8 width to hook the hatband just above the brim.

3. Outline the top of the hat with antique black wool and fill it in.

4. Outline the snowman's head with the light gray herringbone by hooking just slightly inside the drawn line.

5. Fill in the head using the off-white wool.

6. Work the eyes, nose, and mouth with the appropriate colors as you are filling in the face. Use a smaller cut when hooking these features.

7. An easy way to create a #4 cut strip for the mouth is to hold a #8 strip between your fingers and carefully cut it in half (as shown) with your scissors.

8. Next outline the middle and lower part of the snowman's body with the gray herringbone, hooking just slightly inside the line.

9. Fill in the body with the off-white wool, working in the buttons when you get to the appropriate spots.

10. Hook the snowman's arms using the brown texture. Hook directly on the line. The longest, straightest line should be hooked first and then add the smaller twig finger lines afterward.

Hook the Letters

1. Hook the letter S using the blue and white herringbone and following the long continuous curved line. Hook directly on the drawn line.

2. Pull up your loops ¼" high, or to the height that you would normally hook. When you have completed the curved shape of the S, go back and hook the serifs (small lines at the ends of the letter) in a perpendicular line.

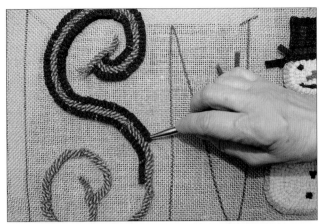

3. Once you get the entire letter S hooked, hook one row of the dark teal blue background around it. The background will hold the shape of the letter while you are working on the next letter. Make sure you hook the background as high as the loops are hooked in the letter.

4. Work the N in the same fashion as the S. Hook the long straight lines of the letter, making a neat angle at the top of the letter.

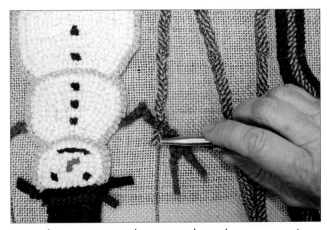

5. When you get to the point where the snowman's arm crosses the letter, pull up the blue herringbone strip and cut it off. Continue with a new strip on the other side of the arm. Do not cross underneath the line of the arm to continue hooking.

6. Hook the serifs on the ends and immediately hook one row of background around the N.

7. Finally, hook the letter W. Hook the long lines first; stop and start your strip when your hooking intersects the snowman's arm. Hook the serifs last, and immediately hook one row of background around the W.

1. Hook one row of background wool around the snowman.

2. Work your background color into all the empty spaces around the letters and snowman. Follow the shapes around the letters and snowman. This will create gently curved repetitive lines, which resemble the ripples that a stone makes when it is dropped into water. This method of filling is called "echoing."

3. I like to hook two straight rows around the outermost perimeter of my rug whenever possible. I think it gives the mat a neat look and a stable foundation for binding the edges. Fill in the rest of the background beyond the letters, and hook in the two straight rows as you go around.

4. I hook a short distance of the two rows and then work my background from the center of the rug out to meet them. Once I get an entire area filled in, I continue for another short distance by hooking the two straight rows along the edge and then work more of the background color until the entire rug is hooked.

5. Once the hooking is completed, turn your rug over and check for any holidays. Steam press your rug both back and front and allow it to dry. Bind the edges. (*Refer to Chapters 6 and 8.*)

CHAPTER 12

A Lesson on Creative Hooking Techniques:
Fancy Flower Basket

MATERIALS
(finished size: 21" x 12½")

- Foundation cloth of your choice, cut to 29" x 21"

- 10" x 17" piece of dark brown plaid wool for the outline of the flower basket

- 11" X 15" piece of golden brown plaid for the flower basket

- 4" x 16" piece of spring green wool for beading

- 3½" x 16" piece of turquoise wool for beading

- 5" x 17" piece of fuchsia plaid wool for flowers

- 3" x 15" piece of purple herringbone wool for flowers

- 3½" x 16" piece of yellow check wool for flowers

- 2" x 16" piece of bright turquoise wool for flowers

- 3½" x 16" piece of orange wool for flowers

- 3" x 16" piece of dark green wool for stems

- 5" x 16" piece of green herringbone wool for leaves

- ³⁄₈ yard of beige plaid and ³⁄₈ yard of khaki plaid (³⁄₄ yard total) wool for the background, cut and mixed together

Manipulating your wool strips into creative stitches is a great way to add a little extra pizzazz to your hooked rug. Here are two popular techniques that rug hookers love to work into their designs. *Beading* is the procedure of hooking two different wool strips at the same time, forming a row of alternating colors. *Quillies* are coiled wool strips that are sewn and attached to your foundation cloth. In *Fancy Flower Basket* I used soft hues that create a subtle glow. Use colors with higher contrast if you like a bolder look.

Cut your wool strips in a #8 size. The wool amounts listed are general estimates. Your needs may vary depending on how high or low you hook.

The finished size of the rug is 21" x 12½". Cutting your foundation cloth to a measurement of 29" x 21" will allow 4" of excess material around each side of the pattern. Transfer the design to the backing of your choice with a waterproof marker. Refer to Chapter 5 on drawing patterns for details. Stretch your pattern tightly over a rug hooking frame or hoop.

Practice the beading technique on a scrap piece of foundation cloth before you start to hook your project.

How to Hook Fancy Flower Basket

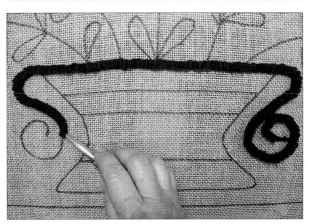

1. Since the basket is the predominant object in the design, hook it first. Using the dark brown plaid wool, outline across the top of the basket and then hook directly on the drawn line to create the handles.

Fancy Flower Basket, 21" x 12½", #8-cut wool on linen. Designed and hooked by Kris Miller, Howell, Michigan, 2014.

Fancy Flower Basket © 2013 Kris Miller, enlarge to 21" x 12½".

2. When the handles are completed, outline the rest of the basket, hooking just inside the line.

3. Immediately work one row of background wool around the basket and the handles to hold their shape.

4. Use the golden brown wool to start filling in the area at the top of the basket. Work horizontally from one side to the other.

5. Hook three straight rows and then hook the next row with the dark brown plaid.

6. Bead the spring green and turquoise wool together below the dark brown row. Work straight across the basket. These two photos show the progression of the beading.

BEADING

Beading is a creative stitch named for its two-toned appearance. Choose two wool strips that are contrasting in color. Decide which color you will hold on the right and on the left. For example, I will hold the blue strip on the right side and the green strip on the left. Paying attention to which side the strips are located will help you keep them in order so they will not become twisted on the bottom of your work. Twisting will not affect the outward appearance of the beading, but it will leave a thick lump underneath your foundation cloth. Hold both strips in your left hand, allow them to hang down loosely side-by-side, and place your left hand underneath your foundation cloth, ready to hook.

1 Push your hook through a hole in the foundation cloth and pull up an end. In my example, I pulled up the green end, which was held on the left.

2 Push your hook down into the very next hole, and pull up the other end, which was my blue wool, located on the right.

3 Underneath your frame, allow your left-hand fingers to push the blue strip over slightly to the right and then grasp only the green wool strip. Push your hook down into the next hole, and pull up a loop of the green wool.

4 Again, using the fingers of your left hand, push the green strip over slightly to the left and grab the blue strip. Skip two holes, push your hook down into the foundation, and pull up a blue loop.

5 Underneath, push the blue strip over slightly to the right, grasp the green strip, skip two holes, and pull a loop of green wool up to the top.

6 Continue hooking in this sequence, forming a row of loops that alternate in color. Occasionally, the loops may lean to one side or the other, but once you hook another row of loops next to the beaded row, the loops will stand up straight again.

7 At the end of a strip, pull up the tail in the next hole. Begin a new strip in the same hole. Pay attention to color. For example, if the blue strip is getting short, pull up its tail right after a hooked green loop and start a new blue strip in the same hole where the previous blue strip ended.

8 Hook the next loop with green wool. Continue working the row for a few stitches and then snip off the tails that were left at the top of your work. Your cut ends will blend in with the rest of the loops and not be noticeable.

9 When you have hooked the beading, flip your foundation over and examine the back. The bottom of the green and blue loops should run parallel to each other. They will be slightly raised but should be smooth and even.

7. When you get to the opposite edge of the basket, end the beading by pulling up the tail of one strip in one hole and pulling the second tail up in the next hole.

8. Hook one row of dark brown wool, another row of beading, followed by another row of dark brown.

9. Continue filling in the basket with the golden brown wool until you reach the lower drawn line.

10. Hook a row of dark brown, a row of beading, and another row of dark brown.

11. Fill in the remaining area at the bottom of the basket with the golden brown wool.

12. Create a quillie circle with the yellow check and orange wool and sew it to the center of the center flower.

Quillie Circles

Quillie circles are sometimes called standing wool circles. I call them "quillies" because the technique reminds me of the old craft of paper rolling called quilling.

Quillie circles are composed of several wool strips that are set on their edges, rolled up, and sewn to the foundation cloth. In order for your quillie circles to fit flush with your hooked loops, you must measure how high you pull up your loops. If you hook approximately ¼" high, a #8 strip will work perfectly for your quillie circles.

1 Cut two #8 strips of wool. Use contrasting colors for the best results. Arrange the two strips so that one is on top of the other and their ends are even.

2 Turn them on their edge and begin to roll both strips into a circle, just like a jelly roll.

3 Roll the quillie circles on a smooth table surface to help even out the edges. When you get to the desired size of the circle, stick a long quilting pin all the way through the roll.

4 Trim off the excess ends. Thread a long needle and begin sewing through the quillie circle.

5 Your thread does not have to be an exact match to the wool colors. Think about the spokes on a wagon wheel and pass the needle through the wool circle in the same pattern. Make 6 or 7 stitches back and forth until you have secured the strips. Do not pull tightly on the thread or you will distort the shape of the circle. When your sewing is completed, knot and cut the thread.

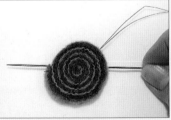

6 Flip the quillie circle over and examine the opposite side. Each side will look a little different. Place your quillie, favorite side up, on your foundation cloth. Sew the outside edges of the quillie circle to your foundation using a whipstitch. Your sewing needle should only come up about halfway into the wool circle and then take another stitch down into the foundation cloth, very close to the base of the circle. Your thread does not need to match perfectly.

7 Once it is securely fastened to the foundation cloth, hook one row of loops closely around the quillie circle.

13. Work one row of fuchsia plaid wool closely around the edge of the quillie circle.

14. Outline the outer perimeter of the flower with the fuchsia plaid and then fill in the empty spaces.

15. Hook the rays of the flower with a single line of purple herringbone.

16. Hook directly on the drawn line, using the dark green wool, to create the flower stem.

17. Hook the leaves in green herringbone wool. Make sure you stay just inside the drawn line when working the leaves so they do not become too large and lose their shape.

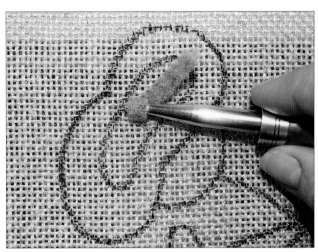

18. To create the center dot of the left center bell-flower, use a strip of bright turquoise wool and pull up an end, hook one loop, then pull up the other end.

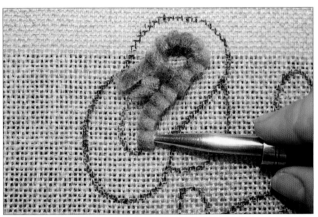

19. Hook an outline of yellow check wool around the center oval and fill in the empty areas.

20. Outline and fill the outer oval petal with orange wool.

21. Fill in the sepal with spring green wool.

22. Then, hook the dark green stem, working directly on the drawn line.

23. Outline and fill the leaves with the green herringbone.

24. Hook the middle dot of the right center flower with the orange wool, pulling up an end, hooking a loop, and pulling up the other end.

25. Immediately hook two circles around the center dot with bright turquoise wool.

26. Work two rows of yellow checked wool around the previously hooked circles.

27. The outer edge of the flower is beaded with orange and spring green wool strips.

28. Work all the way around the perimeter of the flower. When you get back to the starting point, pull up the tail of orange wool in the hole where the orange strip started and pull up the end of the spring green wool in the hole where the spring green strip originally began. Trim off all ends with your scissors so they are flush with the other loops.

29. Your cut ends will not show when the flower is completed.

30. Hook the stems and leaves as you have done for the other flowers.

31. Create a quillie circle with a strip of yellow check wool and the purple herringbone wool. Sew the circle to the center of the far right flower.

32. Immediately hook one row of purple herringbone around the quillie circle.

33. Outline the outermost circle of the flower with fuchsia plaid. Then, fill in the empty space remaining with purple herringbone.

34. Hook the stem and the leaves in the same manner as the other flowers.

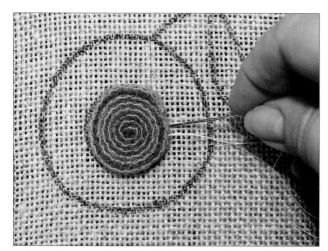

35. Using an orange and a bright turquoise wool strip, make a quillie circle and attach it to the center of the far left flower by sewing it down to the foundation.

36. Closely hook one row of beading around the quillie circle, using the bright turquoise and yellow check wool.

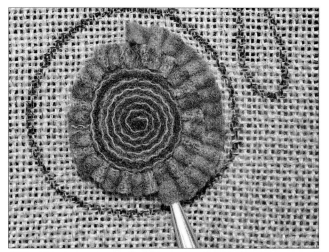

37. Work one row of yellow check around the row of beading, followed by a row of fuchsia plaid.

38. Hook the stem and leaves.

39. Cut and mix the two background plaids. Place them in a plastic bag or container and randomly pick one strip out of the pile. Hook one row of background wool around all of the motifs.

40. When you come to narrow spots, turn your hook sideways while you are pulling up the loop so it will fit in the narrow spot easily.

41. Work around the leaves and stems, filling in the small empty spots.

42. As you fill in the background, simultaneously work the two straight rows along the outermost perimeter of the rug. These rows will give a stable foundation for your binding.

43. When the hooking is completed, turn your rug over and check for holidays. Note that there will be blank spots where the quillie circles were sewn onto the foundation cloth: these areas are not considered holidays.

44. Steam press your rug both back and front and allow it to dry. Bind the edges. (*Refer to Chapters 6 and 8.*)

CHAPTER 13

A Lesson on Hooking Alternative Materials:
Rise and Shine

This is a free-for-all kind of project where you have permission to play and have fun! There are no rules and no limits as to what you can use. Collect a variety of materials in colors and textures that inspire and excite you. Try ribbons, cotton homespun fabric, soft velvet, hosiery and tights, knit sweaters, antique paisley, sheep curls, roving, and novelty yarns with slubs, glitter, or metallic threads.

I have a private stash of yarns, ribbons, paisley, silk chiffon, and other fun treasures that I have saved for "some day." I raided my stash and pulled together colors and textures that I loved and thought would work together for *Rise and Shine*. The materials listed here are only a suggestion. Gather together what you love and unleash your creativity. These instructions are merely a jumping-off point for you to experiment.

The wool and material amounts listed below are general estimates. Your needs may vary depending on how high or low you hook and the types of materials used. You may find it easier to pull up the alternative materials by using a wide-shank hook such as a Hartman or Ritchie Hook. These types of hooks poke a larger hole in the foundation cloth so that you can easily pull bulky materials through.

The finished size of the rug is 11³/₄" x 15". Cutting your foundation cloth to a measurement of 20" x 23" will allow 4" of excess material around each side of the pattern. Transfer the design to the backing of your choice with a waterproof marker. Refer to Chapter 5 on drawing patterns for details. Stretch your pattern tightly over a rug hooking frame or hoop.

MATERIALS (finished size: 11³/₄" x 15")

- Foundation cloth of your choice, cut to 20" x 23"

- 4¹/₂" x 20" piece of antique paisley for the rooster wing (#8.5 cut)

- 1 pair of black sparkly child's tights or similar material for the rooster outline (You can also use a 4" x 16" piece of black wool if desired.)

- 9" x 16" piece of black and white wool (tweed, herringbone, check, or honeycomb texture is suitable) (#8.5 cut) for rooster's body

- 1 strip of antique black wool (#8 cut) for rooster's eye

- 1 strip of cream or pale yellow wool (#8 cut) for rooster's eye

- 2" x 14¹/₂" piece of textured red/orange wool (#8 cut) for beak and legs

- 1" x 16" piece of purple plaid wool (#8 cut) for embellishing rooster's tail

- 3" x 15" piece of dark green wool (#8.5 cut) for the lower ground

- 3" x 16" piece of medium green wool (#8.5 cut) for the middle ground

- 5" x 16" piece of light green plaid wool (#8.5 cut) for the upper ground

- 7" x 16" piece of green cotton fabric that is the same color on both sides, such as homespun

(ripped into ³/₄" strips) for middle ground

- 19" x 16¹/₂" piece of taupe plaid and a 9" x 25" piece of dark beige plaid (#8.5 cut) for the background

- ³/₈ yard of coral/purple plaid (#8 cut) (Use a 14" piece of this wool for hooking two outside border rows and the rest for crocheting around the edge.)

- Collection of coral, ruby, and gold sari ribbons; novelty knitting yarns in green, coral, pink, and metallic gold; dark green dyed sheep curls

Rise and Shine, 11¾" x 15", #8- and 8.5-cut wool, cotton, silk, and alternative materials on linen. Designed and hooked by Kris Miller, Howell, Michigan, 2014.

Rise and Shine, © 2013 Kris Miller, enlarge to 11¾" x 15".

1. Hook the wing of the rooster first since it is on top of the body. Outline the wing and then fill it in.

2. I used a piece of paisley from an antique shawl to hook the wing. If you examine paisley closely, you will notice that the right side (bottom) is smooth with an intricate woven design. On the wrong side (top), there are tiny threads running in one direction.

> ### TIP
>
> *The paisley should be cut in the same direction that the threads run. Use a cutter and only guide small amounts through at one time. Paisley frays and shreds very easily so it is critical that it is cut on the straight of the grain and that you cut it in a strip of #8 width or above. I cut my strips of paisley in a #8.5 width.*

3. Trim any loose threads from the hooked surface.

4. Next outline the rooster's body (you will not need to outline the tail feathers). I used a pair of children's sparkly black tights. Prepare them for hooking by cutting the legs away from the top panty area. Slip one leg over a cardboard tube or cylindrical chip can.

5. Cut across the leg of the tights with a pair of sewing scissors, starting out on a slight angle.

6. Spiral your cutting around the tube to form a continuous strip.

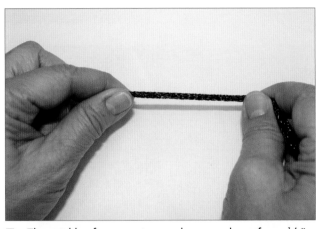

7. The width of your strip can be anywhere from $1/2$" (if the material is thick) to $3/4$" to 1" if the material is thinner. After you cut the strip, grasp a portion of it in each hand and give it a gentle tug. This will stretch the material, causing the edges to curl inward into a tube.

8. Hook the prepared continuous strip just as you would hook a wool strip.

9. Use a little less tension with your left hand and pull your loops up a little higher if the elasticity of the strip causes it to shrink lower than the rest of your loops.

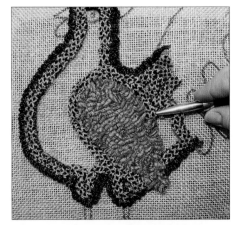

10. Once the rooster outline is completed, use the black and white wool to hook one row around the inside of the chicken body and the wing. Use a #8.5 cut strip to maximize the look of textured pattern in the wool.

11. Hook the rooster's eye next, before the rest of the body is filled in. To form the center dot of the eye, use a strip of antique black wool and pull up an end, hook one loop, and then pull up the other end.

12. Immediately hook the outer circle of the eye with the cream or pale yellow wool, working closely around the black dot you have just hooked.

13. Completely fill in the rest of the rooster's body with the black and white wool.

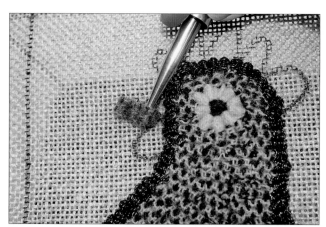

14. Hook the rooster's pointed beak with the textured red/orange wool, using the same technique as described in Chapter 9 for hooking star points.

15. The rooster's wattle and comb are hooked with ruby-colored sari ribbon.

SARI TIP

Hook the sari ribbon just as you would hook a wool strip. Sometimes you will come across a knot in the sari ribbon while you are hooking. You can cut the ribbon where the knot is located and start a new strip, or pull up the ribbon until the knot rests on the bottom of your foundation cloth and just leave it there. The projects I have hooked with sari ribbon are not intended for use on the floor so I am not concerned if there is a lump on the back of my work.

16. After the wattle and comb are hooked, work one row of background wool around the entire rooster's head to define the shape and hold the sari ribbon in place.

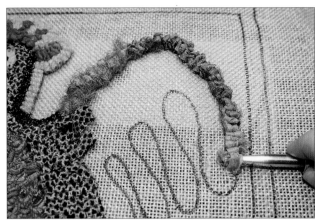

17. Outline the tail feathers and fill them in with the novelty yarns and other alternative materials, hooking in the direction that the feathers would grow. As you hook, you can decide which materials will work best.

18. Use your creativity and place your colors and materials randomly or in any order that is pleasing.

19. Hook ribbon and bulky weight yarn just as you would a wool strip. Thin yarns can be pulled up and hooked in between the rows of wider material.

TIP

Colorful alternate fabrics like ribbon and novelty yarns can add a delightful touch to a hooked rug. Make sure you pull them up high enough so they are visible and not crowded out by the rows of wool next to them. You can also work in colorful bits of wool strips along with your other materials for sparks of interest.

20. When the tail feathers are completely filled in, use the textured red/orange wool to hook the rooster's legs.

21. Hook down to the area where the ground is drawn and pull your ends to the top of your work. You can trim the ends later once the ground is hooked. At this point, I hooked one row of background wool around the entire rooster body to help hold everything in place and define what I had already hooked.

22. Hook the area of the lower ground with the dark green wool. Outline around the shape, staying just inside the drawn line, and then fill it in completely.

23. Outline the middle portion of ground with medium green wool and fill it with green cotton fabric. To create strips from the cotton fabric, measure over 3/4" from the selvedge edge, make a snip in the bottom of the fabric, and rip off the strip. Hook the cotton just as you would a wool strip.

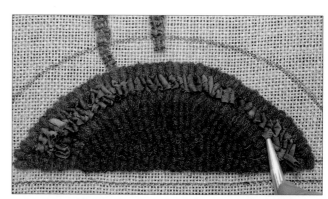

24. For added dimension, pull it up a little higher than the rest of your hooking. If there are stray threads sticking up on the top of your work, simply snip them off with your scissors.

25. Outline and fill the upper layer of ground with light green plaid wool.

26. I pulled up a green nubby novelty yarn in between the hooked rows of the medium and light green wools. Push your rug hook down in between the rows and pull up a loop of yarn. Hook the yarn a little higher than the wool strips so the nubs and texture of the yarn are visible.

1. You can further enhance the lower level of the ground by adding sheep curls, dyed dark green. Sheep curls are easy to hook and should be added after hooking an area. Hold a single curl in your left hand under your foundation cloth. Push your hook down in between two hooked rows and pull up one end of the sheep curl.

2. Adjust it so that approximately ³/₄" to 1" of the end is showing. Poke your hook back down into the next hole of your foundation cloth and bring up a loop.

3. Pull it high enough so that it hangs loosely above the hooked wool strips. Push your rug hook back down between the hooked rows and pull up a second long loop.

4. When you get to the end of the curl, pull it up to the top of your work so that it hangs loosely.

5. Sheep curls will vary in length but you can generally hook an end, two loops, and pull up the other end with one strand. To start a second curl, pull the new end up through the same hole in which the first one ended.

6. Continue hooking long loops until you get to the end of the curl. Work with the curls in this manner until you complete the desired area on your mat. Finish by bringing a curly end up to the top of your work.

Work the Background

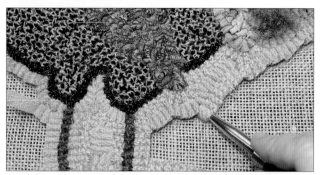

1. Cut and mix the two background wools together. Put them in a plastic bag or container to mix them, then randomly choose a strip. Hooking the background like this will create subtle movement and flow around the design. Follow the contours of the rooster, working out toward the edge.

2. Hook at least one straight row along the edge while you are filling in the background.

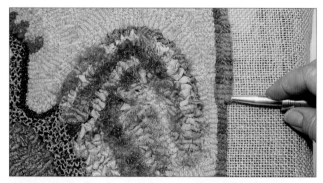

3. Once the background is completed, hook two straight rows of a coordinating plaid or texture around the outer perimeter of the rug to create a small border. The colors of this coordinating wool should contain some of the colors you used in the rooster's tail so that the border relates to the rest of the mat.

4. Turn your rug over and check for holidays. Steam your rug both back and front, and take extra care not to press over the areas that contain the novelty yarns, ribbons, and sheep curls. Allow your mat to dry thoroughly. Sew two rows of preliminary stay stitching around the mat (*see Chapter 6 on finishing*).

Crochet the Edge

The crochet edge finish with wool strips has a handmade rustic look that is perfect for wide cut and primitive rugs. It's a great funky look for *Rise and Shine*. This binding method is fast and fun to do. I have used it many times on my hooked rugs when I have difficulty matching a yarn color to my border. You will always be able to match your edges perfectly because you can crochet with the same wool fabric used to hook your rug or mat. You don't need to have prior knowledge of crochet techniques for this finish.

Use a Hartman or Ritchie hook instead of a crochet hook. The fat handle of the rug hook will be much more comfortable in your hand as you are working. Cut all of your strips in a #8 width. It is important to cut your wool strips as long as possible. A 60" long wool strip will only crochet for 4" along the rug's edge so plan your strips accordingly. It is perfectly acceptable if you cut your wool on the cross grain of the fabric to give you a longer strip.

1. To prepare your mat for a crochet edge, measure 1½" from the last row of hooking and make a mark with a permanent marker or pencil.

2. Continue marking all the way around the perimeter. Following the marked lines, carefully cut away the excess backing using a sharp pair of scissors.

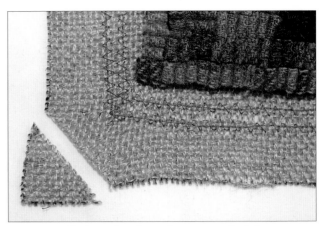

3. Snip off about ½" from the points of all four corners.

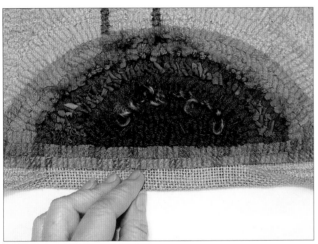

4. Working from the right side of the mat, fold the trimmed foundation cloth in half.

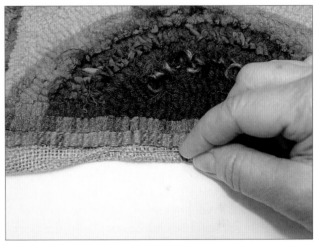

5. Fold the edge in half again, pinning it in place as you go until you get close to a corner.

6. First fold in the corner so that the cut end is lying flat against the corner loop of your hooking.

7. Then, fold the foundation in half on either side of the corner and pin it in place.

8. The corners should be aligned but do not have to form a perfect point.

9. With a sewing needle and thread, baste all the pinned edges and corners with a running stitch.

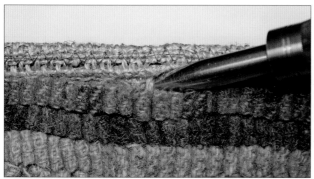

10. Start crocheting in an inconspicuous spot, generally on the lower left hand side of the mat. Do not start in a corner. Work from the right side of your mat with your hook in your right hand and a long strip of wool in your left hand behind the mat. Push your hook down into a hole in the foundation cloth below the basted edge. You will be going through only a single layer.

11. You want to get close to the feet of the hooked loops but do not go in between them. Pull up a loop, making it as high as the basted fold.

12. Allow a 3" tail of your strip to hang behind your work. Bring the wool strip up from the back and wrap it around the end of your rug hook.

13. Pull the strip through the loop on your hook. You will have formed one loop.

14. Insert your hook down into the foundation again, close to the feet of the hooked loops and two or three holes away from the first stitch.

15. Wrap the wool strip around your hook and then pull up another loop, making it as high as the folded edge. You now have two loops on your hook.

16. Bring the wool strip up from the back, and wrap it around the tip of your rug hook.

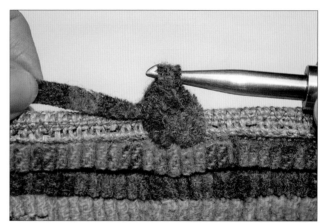

17. Pull the wool strip through the two loops on your hook. This may seem awkward at first; use your fingers to coax the strip through the loops. You will end up with one loop on your hook. You have formed your first single crochet stitch.

18. Push your hook back down into the foundation, two or three holes away from the last stitch.

19. Pull up a loop from behind; pull it as high as the folded edge (two loops on the hook).

20. Wrap the wool strip around your hook and pull it through the two loops (now there is one loop on your hook). Continue with this procedure until you come to the end of your strip.

21. Before you join a new strip, leave the end of the old strip lying along the basted edge. Trim it to about 2".

22. Hold the new strip behind your work. Push your hook through the foundation cloth and pull up a loop from the new strip.

23. Allow 3" of the new tail to hang loosely behind your work. Continue to crochet with the new wool strip, encasing the tail from the old strip while you are working. I do not encase both the new and old tails together because it creates too much bulk. The loose hanging ends will be woven in later.

24. As you approach a corner, make sure that the strip you are working with is still long enough to crochet around it. You do not want to run out before you completely turn the corner, so start a new strip if necessary. Crochet right up to the corner; work three single crochet stitches in the same corner hole, fanning out the wool stitches to cover the corner completely.

25. Once the three corner crochet stitches are completed, begin working down the next side.

26. When you have crocheted completely around the perimeter of the mat, join the crochet stitches together by pulling the end of your current wool strip through the last loop formed.

27. This will lock it in place and prevent your stitches from unraveling. Thread the end of the wool strip through the large eye of a tapestry needle and thread it through a few of the previous crochet loops.

28. Cut the strip even with your work. Weave in the loose ends on the back of your work by threading the ends through the large eye of a tapestry needle and pulling the tails through a few stitches on the back of your work. Trim the ends evenly.

29. Steam press the edges of your mat, both front and back (*refer to Chapter 6*).

CHAPTER 14

A Lesson on Proddy:
Maisy

MATERIALS
(finished size: 11" x 8½")

- Foundation cloth of your choice, cut to 20" x 20"

- 5" x 17" piece of antique black wool (#6 and 8 cuts) for the sheep's face, ears, and legs

- One strip of gold/brown wool (#8 cut) for the eye

- 4 different light neutral textures of wool, the size of each should be approximately 6" x 16" (³/₄" wide strips), for proddy sheep

- 24" x 16½" piece of spring green plaid wool (#8 cut) for background

- 9" x 16" piece of darker spring green wool (#8 cut) for border

Proddy is a rug making technique that is prevalent in England and has become very popular in the United States and Canada. Instead of continuous loops, individually cut wide strips are poked or pulled through the foundation cloth to create a luxurious pile. The proddy technique can be done as an entire rug or be combined with rug hooking to enhance and provide added dimension to a design. Flowers, animals, and landscapes are all candidates for proddy accents.

Not only is proddy easy to do, but you can also use all different types of materials. Fabrics that are normally unsuitable for rug hooking are usable in proddy rugs. Synthetic blends, thin woolens, thick textures, blankets, knit sweaters, and even plastic shopping bags have all been used.

There are special tools for making proddy rugs, but if you are embellishing just a portion of your hooked project, a rug hook with a wide shank is all that you need. I recommend a Hartman hook or Ritchie hook with at least an 8 mm shaft. The wide shaft can poke a big hole in the foundation cloth and that will make it much easier to pull up your proddy strip.

Traditionally, prodded rugs were made by lacing a rug pattern to a large wooden frame, wrong side up, and poking the cut fabric pieces through a foundation cloth. However, I find when working on small projects or when using proddy strips as an enhancement in a few select areas of the design, it is easier to work from the right side of the pattern using a rug hook and a frame. Therefore, all the proddy strips in *Maisy* will be worked from the front of the mat.

Your proddy project will be much more interesting if you mix several different textures and values together. Even though our perception of creating a sheep might be to use all white tones, you should mix other colors to obtain a pleasing look. Real-life sheep that spend their days out in a pasture can be dirty little critters and are rarely pure white. I like to combine at least four neutral colors together. For example: off-white, beige, cream, and light gray. Use plaids, checks, and stripes along with solids. When you mix all the strips together and work them into the design, you will give a nice depth and variety to your sheep's fleece.

Read the entire instructions before cutting your wool. The wool amounts listed are general estimates. Your needs may vary depending on how high or low you hook.

The finished size of the rug is 11" x 8½". Cutting your foundation cloth to a measurement of 20" x 20" will allow more than 4" of excess material around each side of the pattern so it will be easier to fit in your frame or hoop. Transfer the design to the backing of your choice with a waterproof marker. Refer to Chapter 5 on drawing patterns. Stretch your pattern tightly over a rug hooking frame or hoop.

Maisy, 11" x 8½", #8-cut and hand-cut wool on linen. Designed and hooked by Kris Miller, Howell, Michigan, 2014.

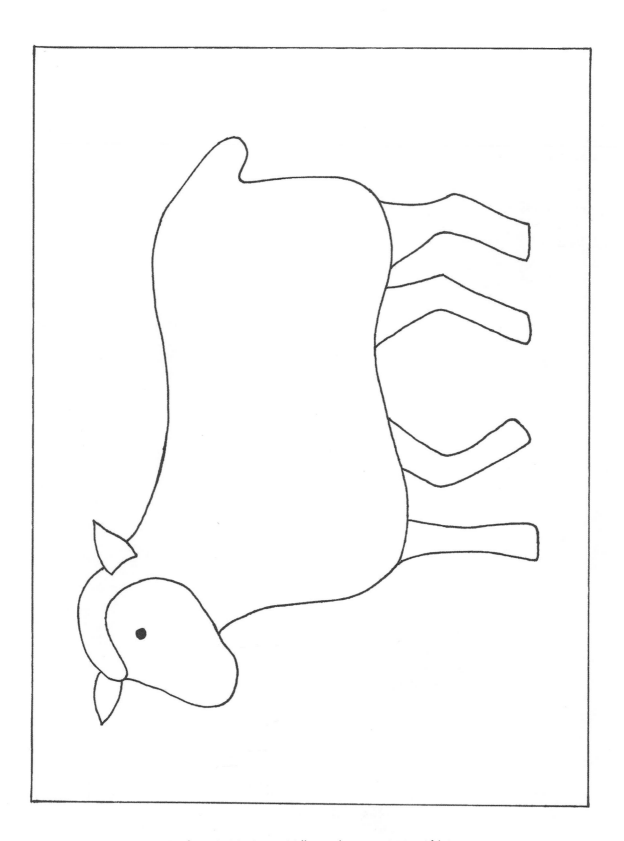

Maisy, © 2013 Kris Miller, enlarge to 11" x 8½".

Hook the Face

1. Hook the sheep's face first before you put in your proddy strips. Outline the sheep's face by using the antique black wool cut in a #8 width.

2. Fill in the head, working the eye as you are hooking. Pull up an end, hook a loop, and pull up the other end.

3. Once the face is completed, hook both ears. Leave a space between the face and ears so you can work a row of proddy strips over the top of the head.

Decide what width and length strip size is appropriate for your project. Generally, I cut my proddy strips ³/₄" wide and 2¹/₂" to 3" long. You can adjust these measurements to fit your specific project.

1 For *Maisy*, you will be prodding with a ³/₄"-wide strip. Using a tape measure, measure over ³/₄" and make  a snip in the edge of the wool. Rip the strip with your hands. I like the effect of the ragged edge but if you would like a clean cut, use a rotary cutter, clear ruler, and a self-healing mat to cut your strips.

2 Lay your ripped or cut strip along the tape measure. You will be using a 2¹/₂" long strip of wool to prod the sheep (using a longer strip will make your sheep too shaggy). Cut your strip at every 2¹/₂" interval.

3 Shape the ends of your strips to suit your project or leave them square. I like to round off the sharp corners of the strips when prodding sheep to give a nice soft 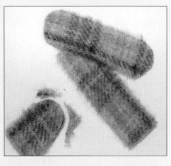 feeling to the fleece. Fold the strip in half. Using your scissors, nip off the points and round off the ends. The rounded ends don't have to be perfect so don't worry if they are a little uneven.

4 Cut and prepare a quantity of strips so you can work on your proddy project without having to constantly stop to cut more. It's handy to keep them in a bowl or  basket close at hand while you are working.

5 Work from the right side of your work with the design facing you. Hold your proddy strip underneath your frame or hoop just as if you were going to hook a wool strip. Push your rug hook down into the foundation so most of the shank has passed through the foundation cloth and it makes a big hole.

6 Grab one end of the proddy strip with your hook and bring half of it up to the top of your work.

7 Count over five threads and poke your hook back down into your foundation cloth.

8 Pull up the other half of the proddy strip. Use your fingers to adjust the strip and make both ends even.

9 Hold a new proddy strip underneath your foundation cloth. Push your hook down into the same hole that the previous strip ended and pull up one end of your new strip. You will have two ends coming up in the same hole.

10 Count over five threads, push your hook down, grab the other end of the second strip and pull it up to the top of your work.

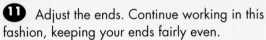

11 Adjust the ends. Continue working in this fashion, keeping your ends fairly even.

12 When you prod around a curve, it's hard to count five threads accurately so estimate about 1/4" from the last row. For each new row, count over five threads from the row you have just worked.

13 After prodding several rows, look at the back. The strips should look flat and smooth with no protruding lumps or large gaps where the foundation is showing between the proddy strips.

1. Begin prodding by outlining around the sheep's body, making sure to stay just inside the drawn line as you are working.

2. Use a mixture of the four different neutral textures chosen randomly as you are prodding. You may find it easier to pull the proddy strips up through the foundation if you fold them in half lengthwise first.

3. When you get to the sheep's head, prod one row over the top of its head. For this area only, I cut the proddy strips in a slightly shorter size of 1/2" x 2". The face and ears will show up a little better and not be obscured by a longer length.

4. Prod around the sheep's body, working each new row approximately five threads away from the last one.

5. As the body becomes filled in, you may have to use your fingers to push away some of the previous proddy strips to work in the new ones.

6. Once your proddy sheep is completed, flip your piece over and examine the back. Make sure there are no large areas where your foundation cloth is exposed, and check that all the strips are lying smooth and flat.

7. Hook the sheep's legs. Push back the proddy strips with your hand to hook in the first loop or so. I hooked the legs with a #8- and a #6-cut strip so I could fill in the space properly, but use whatever cut you are most comfortable working with.

Add the Background

1. Fill in the background, using the spring green plaid. Hook one row around the prodded sheep body first. Push the  proddy strips out of the way as you are working. Use small quilting clips or binder clips to help hold the strips upright and away from your hooking.

2. Continue to fill in the background, following the contours and shapes of the sheep.

3. As you get closer to the edge, hook two straight rows of the darker spring green wool for a short distance around the outer perimeter of the mat.

4. Fill in the small openings and empty spaces between the sheep and the border with the lighter spring green wool. Continue hooking until you have filled in the entire background and border.

5. Once the hooking is completed, turn your mat over and check for any holidays. Carefully steam press the hooked areas and edges of your mat, both front and back, but do not press the prodded area. Instead, give it a light shot of steam to fluff it up. Allow the mat to dry thoroughly and bind the edges. (*Refer to Chapters 6 and 8.*)

CHAPTER 15

A Lesson on Fine-Cut Pictorials:
Kurtz's Barn

The style of this small pictorial is impressionistic; it captures the image of an everyday scene without providing a lot of detail. Just like a painter's brushstroke, the direction of your hooking will suggest direction and movement. Think of this technique as painting with wool. Shading and using color values are important aspects in making a successful pictorial.

I live on a small acreage hobby farm where we keep angora goats, sheep, and two Suri alpacas. Our dear friends live on a larger farm nearby, and we buy our hay from them. Their hay barn has been used for many years, originally built by Paul's father when he ran a successful dairy. After I finished my pictorial, I realized that the barn I hooked looked very similar to the Kurtz's barn. It has a little window on the second story where hay is hauled up for storage or thrown down to feed the animals. Therefore, my mat is dedicated to and named after our friend's old beloved barn.

The wool amounts listed are general estimates. Your needs may vary depending on how high or low you hook.

The actual size of the pattern is 7½" x 9". When you hook two straight rows as a border around the outside of the mat, the finished size will be 8¼" x 10". Monk's cloth, rug warp, or linen specifically woven for fine cut wool is recommended for this project. Cutting your foundation cloth to a measurement of 20" x 20" will allow more than 4" of excess material around each side of the pattern so it will be easier to fit in your frame or hoop. Transfer the design to the backing of your choice with a waterproof marker. Refer to Chapter 5 on drawing patterns. Stretch your pattern tightly over a rug hooking frame or hoop. For best results, choose a rug hook that is compatible with hooking fine cut strips, such as a fine or medium sized hook.

MATERIALS (finished size: 8¼" x 10")

- Foundation cloth, cut to 20" x 20"
- 1½" x 16" piece of overdyed black wool (#4 cut) for the sheep faces and ears
- 3" x 15" piece of mottled white (#4 and 5 cuts) for sheep bodies
- 1½" x 16" piece of tan/taupe/brown plaid wool (#6 cut) for fence
- 4" x 16½" piece of gray striped wool (#5 cut) for barn roof
- 1" x 15" piece of dark gray wool (#5 cut) for roof shadow line of barn

- 1"x 16" piece of charcoal wool (#5 cut) for hay loft window
- 3" x 16" piece of overdyed dark red wool (#5 cut) for side of barn
- 4" x 16" piece of overdyed medium red wool (#5 cut) for side of barn
- 1" x 16" piece of brown wool (#4 and 5 cuts) for tree trunk and branches
- Assorted pieces of light, medium, and dark green wool, including olive green and brown (#4 and 5 cuts) for vegetation, ground, and tree, totaling approximately 14" x 16"

- 2-3 strips of dull gold (#5 cut) for wildflowers
- 9" x 16" piece of light blue spot-dyed wool (#4 and 5 cuts) for sky
- 5" x 16" piece of gold and olive green check (#5 cut) for inner border line
- 5" x 17" piece of olive/brown plaid (#5 cut) for outer border line

Kurtz's Barn, 8¼" x 10", #4-, 5-, and 6-cut wool on monk's cloth.
Designed and hooked by Kris Miller, Howell, Michigan, 2014.

Kurtz's Barn, © 2014 Kris Miller, enlarge to 8¼" x 10".

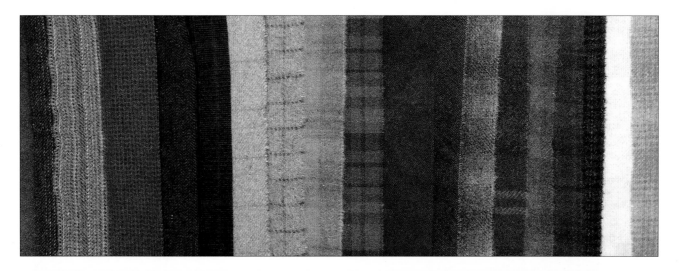

Hook the Sheep

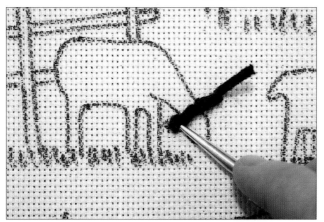

1. Begin by hooking the sheep faces. Use the overdyed black wool to hook the ears while working straight across the head.

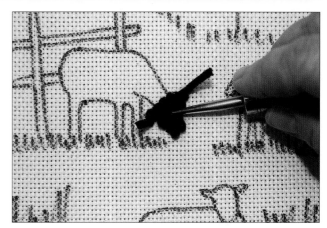

2. Hook around the face and fill the empty space in the middle, continuing to use the black wool.

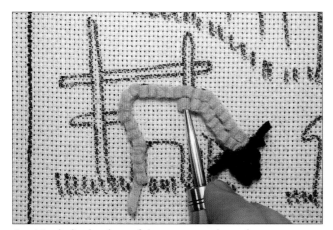

3. Hook the bodies of the two standing sheep in horizontal rows, starting from the head and working along the neck and back toward the tail. Use a #5 width.

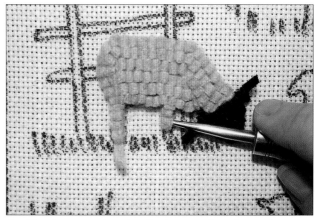

4. The legs are then hooked vertically, also with a #5-cut strip.

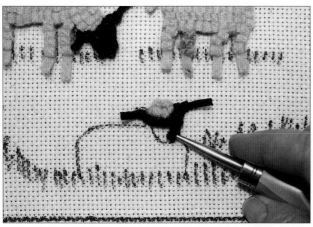

5. As you are hooking the resting sheep's face, add a few loops of mottled white wool, cut in a #4 width, to the top of its head.

6. Work one row of mottled white wool, cut in a #5 width, along its back and then hook the rest of the rows vertically. Hook the sheep's body in such a way that you are allowing a few small open spaces in between the rows of loops at the bottom. You will come back to these spots later to add some blades of grass.

Hook the Fence and the Barn

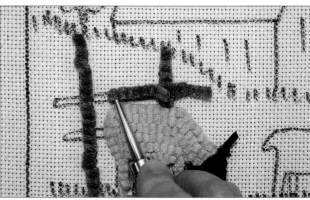

1. Hook the fence behind the sheep with the tan/taupe/brown plaid wool. You only need one row of hooked loops to fill in between the drawn lines.

2. Work the long vertical posts first and then hook the rails. Do not cross underneath your loops to hook the rails. When you come to the fence post, pull up your strip, cut it off, and then begin a new strip of wool on the other side of the fence post.

3. Hook the barn roof with the gray striped wool, cut in a #5 width. The stripes perfectly imitate the look of an old metal roof. Begin at the farthest side next to the tree and hook from the drawn line at the top down to the bottom in a single row.

4. Do not cut your ends yet. Hook about halfway across the roof. Now begin working some rows of the roofing from the front of the barn toward the back. These two areas will eventually meet at a small wedge shape that you must fill in at the top of the roof when all the rows are completed.

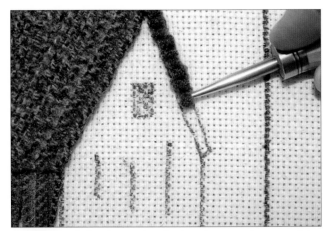

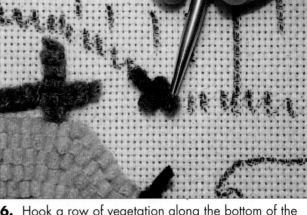

5. The roof shadow is hooked with a single row of the dark gray wool. Start at the top of the roof and work down to the bottom of the drawn line.

6. Hook a row of vegetation along the bottom of the barn. Choose three or four different dark green values of wools in a #5 width. Hook these in little bundles of color, turning your hook in different directions as you pull up the loops so that they do not form a straight line. For instance, pull up an end, hook three or four loops, then pull up the tail and cut it off.

7. At the same time, turn your hook as you are pulling up these loops so that each one is at a slight angle to the previous loop

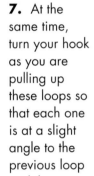

and they are not all facing in the same direction. Begin another strip of a different green color and only hook five or six loops, all angled in different directions. Continue in this manner across the bottom of the barn and out to the edge of the mat, varying the color of wool and the number and direction of the loops.

8. Hook the short side of the barn with the dark red wool, working vertically from top to bottom and using a #5 cut. Trim the tails left from hooking the roof as you go along. Work the dark red wool down in between the loops of vegetation.

9. Hook the hayloft window first, before filling in the larger wall of the barn. Work two short vertical rows with the charcoal wool.

10. Hook the larger side of the barn with the medium red wool. Fill vertically from the corner of the barn all the way over to the other side, working from the top of the building to the bottom. Hook around the window.

1. Hook the tree next. Hook the trunk and a few tree branches with the brown wool in a #4 cut. For best results, do not connect the branches and the trunk.

2. Cut a variety of medium and dark green wools in a #4 cut to use for the leaves. Hook these in small bundles of various green colors, turning your hook in random direcions in the same way that you hooked the vegetation line in front of the barn. Leave a few small unhooked areas. Fill these spots with just a few loops of #4-cut light blue spot-dyed wool. When viewing a tree from a distance in real life, the sky will show through some of the leaves.

3. Hook mostly dark values of green in the bottom of the tree and along the roofline of the barn.

4. Fill in the sky along the bottom of the tree and the horizon line.

5. Take your mat off of your frame and step back to get a good look at your progress. Make adjustments to anything that doesn't look right. For instance, I had hooked a bit too many "sky holes" in my tree, which made it look very lacey, and the tree began to lose its realistic shape. I corrected this by pulling out a few loops of the light blue and refilling them with green leaf wool.

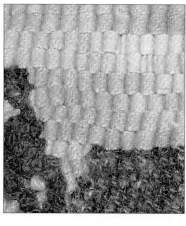

6. Fill in the sky area with #5-cut light blue spot-dyed wool. Since the sky does not take up much area on the mat, I chose to hook it in straight rows. The straight direction also suggests a feeling of calmness and serenity. I began close to the barn roof so I could cut off the ends of the gray striped strips as I worked.

When you fill background with rows that are hooked straight, there will also be a continuous row of cut ends at the edge of the mat. All these ends will line up and become very noticeable. So as not to draw attention away from the design of your rug, hide or bury the ends of the wool strips. Burying ends takes a little extra time but gives great results.

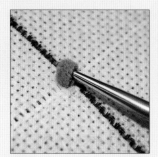  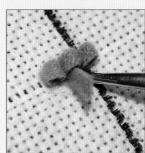 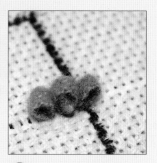

1 First, push your hook down into a hole in your foundation that is next to the drawn border line on the edge of your pattern. Pull up a loop, but do not pull up the tail.

2 Allow ¾" of the end to hang below your work. Hook two more loops as you normally would. You will have three loops. With your left hand, grasp the end hanging below your foundation cloth. Go back to the second loop and poke your hook down directly inside of it.

3 Scoop up the end that you are holding in your left hand and pull it up so that it is coming through the middle of the second loop.

4 Trim the end with your scissors and tuck it back up into the second loop, hiding it. Don't worry if the end happens to poke out a little bit because it will be hidden when you hook the row next to it.

Hooking the Grass

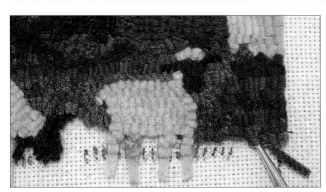

1. Use the darkest values of green closer to the barn, working in the medium and light values as you get toward the bottom of the mat to suggest depth and dimension. Hook with gently sloping lines rather than hooking straight across, mixing the length and color of the strips.

2. The sheep need shadows of darker green below their legs to anchor them to the ground. A fun way to create a little texture and visual interest is to raise your loops in this area. Hook a variety of medium to dark green values, short strips, and crooked loops, pulling them about twice as high as the rest of your hooking to resemble tall grass. Work tall loops around the sheep legs and the areas beyond the sheep.

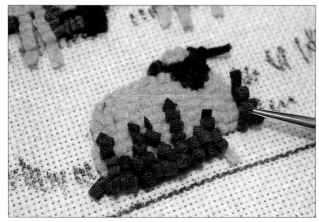

3. When hooking the tall grass around the resting sheep, work the loops up into the spaces you left previously.

4. Vary the amount of the tall grass and trim your ends even with the tallest loops. Once your tall grass has been hooked in, fill around it with rows of normal hooking, following a gentle curve.

5. Work in a few gold loops between the blades of tall grass to suggest wild flowers. I used a dull gold. Don't overdo this accent, so just pull up an end, hook one loop, and then pull up the other end. Place the flowers randomly throughout the grassy area.

6. Completely fill in the grass area around the sheep.

7. Consider hooking a small border around your mat when you are finished. This frames the picture and provides a stable edge for binding. Hook one row of gold and olive green check directly around the outside edge, followed by a row of olive/brown plaid wool.

8. Take your finished mat off of your frame, step back and examine your hooking. Are any objects disappearing into the background or "floating"? Do you need to adjust some of your loops? Make any changes now.

9. Turn your rug over and check for holidays. Steam press your rug on both back and front and allow it to dry. Bind the edges. (*Refer to Chapters 6 and 8.*)

Glossary of Rug Hooking Terms

analogous colors. Colors that are next to each other on the color wheel.

antique black. A color dyed over various types of wool to look like old faded black fabric. It is never a true black color and most often mottled. Dyes used in Antique Black may include browns, dark greens, black, and sometimes deep red.

as-is wool/fabric. Fabric used in its original color and has never been dyed.

backing. See **foundation cloth**.

beading. A decorative stitch that is formed by hooking two different strips of wool at the same time, creating a single row with alternating colored loops.

color triangle. The use of a certain color in three different places on your rug. This causes your eye to move around the rug design and creates balance and interest. There can be more than one color triangle in your rug design.

complementary colors. Colors that are opposite each other on the color wheel. For example, red and green are complementary colors.

crossover. An area on the underneath side of the rug where a strip of wool has been carried over the back of other loops to be hooked in a new area. This creates a lump

on the back of the rug that will most likely wear out prematurely from normal use on the floor.

cutter blades/heads. Metal wheels or cartridges that are specially made to fit into a fabric cutter and whose function is to cut wool into specifically sized strips.

directional hooking. Hooking wool strips in such a way that it creates movement or suggests the shape of an object. For example, hooking in the direction that fur grows on an animal or the way that water flows in an ocean.

echoing/echo hooking. A technique for filling in the background of a rug by hooking around and around the contours of the design elements, creating gently curved repetitive lines. The appearance of this technique may be compared to the ripples that are formed when a stone is dropped into water.

fabric cutter. A mechanical machine most often operated with a hand crank. It may stand on its own or clamp to a table or flat surface. Wool fabric pieces are guided through the machine in order to cut specific-sized strips.

foundation cloth. A loosely woven fabric which strips of wool or other fabrics are pulled through to create a rug. The most common types of foundation cloth are burlap, monk's cloth, or linen. Also called **backing**.

frame. A square, rectangular, or round device that holds foundation cloth taut, usually with gripper strips.

gripper strips. A rubber strip, usually $1^{1}/4$" wide, that is imbedded with fine sharp wire bristles. They are fastened to the top surface of a rug hooking frame and are used to hold foundation cloth taut.

hit and miss/hit or miss. A random placement of colors and stripes, most commonly hooked in straight lines. The strips are hooked in such a way that strips of the same color are not next to each other. Hit and miss can include only the colors used in the main design of your rug, or it can include additional colors besides what was used in the rug.

holiday. A spot on a rug where no loops were hooked. Holidays are most often evident when examining a rug from the wrong side.

hook-in. A one-day event where a large group of rug hookers gather together to work on their projects and socialize. There are usually refreshments, door prizes, a rug show, and vendors.

marrying. Combining several colors of wool in a pot of water without any dye and allowing them to simmer for a length of time. This causes the colors to bleed and blend together in a harmonious way. This is a great technique used for creating backgrounds.

narrow cut. Strips of wool or fabric that are between #2 ($^2/_{32}$") and #5 ($^5/_{32}$"). These strips give greater detail and are most often used in fine shading.

overdyed wool/overdyed fabric. Fabric that has had its color altered or changed by dyeing, either by chemical or natural dyes (tea, plants, etc). Some methods associated with overdyeing include spot dyed, mottled, gradation dyed, casserole dyed, and dip dyed.

packing. The process of hooking loops too close together, forming a tight pile and consequently causing rippling, buckling, or stiffness in the rug.

padula. An imaginary flower not found in nature.

primary colors. Red, blue, and yellow. These three colors are the basis for all the other colors on the color wheel.

primitive. A simple, naïve, folk art style of rug hooking. Color and size of the design subject do not matter.

quillie. A decorative technique in which two different colored wool strips are set on their side and rolled up like a jelly roll to form a spiraled circle. The spiraled circle is sewn through the middle with a needle and thread to hold its shape. It is then sewn down to the foundation cloth before hooking loops around it. Quillies can be used to enhance a rug's design by adding whimsical elements such as flower centers, buttons, spooky eyes, or spots on animals. Also called **standing wool circles**.

wide cut. Strips of wool or fabric that are at least #6 ($^6/_{32}$") or larger and are often associated with primitive designs.

prodding/proddy. A technique where fabric is cut into short wide strips and poked through the back of the foundation cloth with a special tool to form a long shaggy pile on the front. In some instances, proddy may also be worked from the right side of the rug.

recycled wool. Wool fabric that was previously used in another form and originally came from a garment, blanket, etc.

reverse hooking. Pulling out your strips, most often to correct an error. Also called **ripping**.

ripping. See **reverse hooking**.

rug camp/rug school. A retreat or gathering of rug makers that includes instruction from a teacher, room & board, and some meals. Rug camp usually lasts from 3 to 5 days.

rug hook. The tool used to pull fabric strips through a foundation cloth. It often looks like a crochet hook set into a wooden or metal handle. The hook comes in different sizes from fine (smallest) to primitive (largest).

shading. The process of hooking similar, graduated colors together in a design to obtain depth, dimension, and a realistic look to an object.

spark/poison. An unusual or unexpected color hooked into a rug, usually done in small areas for effect.

standing wool circles. See **quillies**.

strip. a piece of fabric that is cut into a certain width and length and used for creating loops, or the pile of a rug. Strips must always be cut on the straight of the grain of the fabric.

swatches. A set of wool pieces that are dyed into graduated colors, usually from light to dark.

tail. The end of a fabric strip that is pulled up to the top of your work and is later trimmed off.

textured wool. Wools that are tweeds, herringbones, plaids, checks, stripes, or unusual weaves.

thrum/snippet. The short ends, or tails which are trimmed off your rug and are discarded.

value. The relative lightness or darkness of a color.

whipping. To completely wrap and cover the edge of a finished hooked piece with wool yarn, fabric strips, or other materials.

worms/noodles. A term to describe leftover cut strips from a previous rug hooking project.

Resources

PUBLICATIONS

- **ATHA (Association of Traditional Rug Hooking Artists)**
  www.atharugs.com

- **Rug Hooking Magazine**
  Ampry Publishing
  3400 Dundee Rd, Suite 220
  Northbrook, IL 60062
  www.rughookingmagazine.com

- **The Wool Street Journal LLC**
  P.O. Box 727
  Colorado Springs, CO 80901
  www.woolstreetjournal.com

RUG HOOKING PATTERNS AND SUPPLIES

- **Cynthia Norwood**
  11001 Swelfling Terrace
  Austin, TX 78737
  canorw@aol.com
  Supplier of antique paisley
  pieces

- **Hill Country Rug Works**
  Bea Brock
  409 Woodcrest Drive
  Kerrville, TX 78028
  www.hillcountry-rugworks.com
  Patterns

- **Holly Hill Designs**
  Susan Quicksall
  3420 County Road 315
  Oglesby, TX 76523
  www.hollyhilldesigns.net
  Patterns and dye book

- **PRO Chemical & Dye**
  P.O. Box 14
  Somerset, MA 02726
  www.prochemical.com
  PRO WashFast Acid Dyes

- **The Red Saltbox**
  Wendy Miller White
  503 South Brady Street
  Attica, IN 47918
  www.theredsaltbox.com
  Patterns

- **Spruce Ridge Studios LLC**
  Kris Miller
  1786 N. Eager Road
  Howell, MI 48855
  www.spruceridgestudios.com
  Patterns and rug hooking
  supplies

- **Star Rug Company**
  Maria Barton
  6191 Link Dr.
  Indian River, MI 49749
  www.starrugcompany.com
  Patterns

- **W. Cushing & Co.,**
  Box 351
  Kennebunkport, ME 04046
  www.wcushing.com
  Cushing dyes and rug hooking
  supplies

- **Woolley Fox LLC**
  Barb Carroll
  132 Woolley Fox Lane
  Ligonier, PA 15658
  www.woolleyfox.com
  Patterns and Ritchie hooks

FABRIC CUTTERS

- **Bee Line Art Tools**
  PO Box 130
  Bettendorf, IA 52722
  www.beeline-townsend.com
  Fabric cutters

- **Bolivar Cutters**
  P.O. Box 539
  Bridgewater
  Nova Scotia
  Canada B4V 2X6
  www.bolivarcutter.com
  Fabric cutters

- **Harry Fraser Co.**
  498 Trot Valley Road
  Stuart, VA 24171
  www.fraserrug.com
  Bliss and Fraser 500 fabric
  cutters

WOOL SUPPLIERS

- **Heavens To Betsy**
  46 Route 23
  Claverack, NY 12513
  www.heavens-to-betsy.com
  Wool yardage

- **The Wool Studio**
  328 Tulpehocken Ave
  West Reading, PA 19611
  www.thewoolstudio.com
  Wool yardage

- **The Dorr Mill Store**
  P.O. Box 88
  Guild, NH 03754-0088
  www.dorrmillstore.com
  Wool yardage, Hartman hooks,
  and rug hooking supplies

ON-LINE GROUPS AND PUBLICATIONS

- *Gene Shepherd's Internet Rug Camp*
  www.geneshepherd.com

- *Rug Hooking Daily*
  www.rughookingdaily.ning.com

- *Rug Hooking Magazine*
  www.rughookingmagazine.com

- *The Welcome Mat*
  www.thewelcomemat.ning.com

FURTHER READING

- Carroll, Barbara, and Emma Lou Lais, **American Primitive Hooked Rugs: A Primer for Recreating Antique Rugs.** Kennebunkport, Maine: Wildwood Press, 1999.

- Close, Lesley Mary, **Hooked Rug Storytelling: The Art of Heather Ritchie.** Atglen, PA: Schiffer Publishing Ltd., 2011.

- **Finishing Hooked Rugs: Favorite Techniques From the Experts.** Mechanicsburg, PA: Stackpole Books, 2013.

- Green, Jane Halliwell, **Pictorial Hooked Rugs.** Mechanicsburg, PA: Stackpole Books, 2009.

- Kopp, Joel, and Kate Kopp, **American Hooked and Sewn Rugs: Folk Art Underfoot.** New York: E.P. Dutton & Co. Inc., 1975.

- McDermet, Kris; Manges Christine; and Tobias, Dianne; **Combining Rug Hooking & Braiding: Basics, Borders, & Beyond.** Atglen, PA: Schiffer Publishing Ltd., 2011.

- Norwood, Cynthia Smesny, **Creating an Antique Look in Hand-Hooked Rugs,** Mechanicsburg, PA: Stackpole Books, 2008.

- Shepherd, Gene, **Prepared to Dye; Dyeing Techniques for Fiber Artists.** Mechanicsburg, PA: Stackpole Books, 2013.

- Shepherd, Gene, **Prodded Hooking For a Three-Dimensional Effect.** Mechanicsburg, PA: Stackpole Books, 2008.

- Turbayne, Jessie A. **Hooked Rug Treasury.** Atglen, PA: Schiffer Publishing Ltd., 1997.